THE CHRYSOSTOM BIBLE
A Commentary Series for Preaching and Teaching
Colossians & Philemon: A Commentary

THE CHRYSOSTOM BIBLE
A Commentary Series for Preaching and Teaching

Colossians & Philemon: A Commentary

Paul Nadim Tarazi

OCABS PRESS
ST PAUL, MINNESOTA 55124
2010

THE CHRYSOSTOM BIBLE
COLOSSIANS & PHILEMON: A COMMENTARY

Copyright © 2010 by
Paul Nadim Tarazi

ISBN 1-60191-013-4

All rights reserved.

PRINTED IN THE UNITED STATES OF AMERICA

Other Books by the Author

I Thessalonians: A Commentary

Galatians: A Commentary

The Old Testament: An Introduction

Volume 1: Historical Traditions, revised edition

Volume 2: Prophetic Traditions

Volume 3: Psalms and Wisdom

The New Testament: An Introduction

Volume 1: Paul and Mark

Volume 2: Luke and Acts

Volume 3: Johannine Writings

Volume 4: Matthew and the Canon

The Chrysostom Bible

Genesis: A Commentary

Philippians: A Commentary

Romans: A Commentary

Land and Covenant

The Chrysostom Bible
Colossians & Philemon: A Commentary

Copyright © 2010 by Paul Nadim Tarazi
All rights reserved.

ISBN 1-60191-013-4

Published by OCABS Press, St. Paul, Minnesota.
Printed in the United States of America.

Books are available through OCABS Press at special discounts for bulk purchases in the United States by academic institutions, churches, and other organizations. For more information please email OCABS Press at press@ocabs.org.

Abbreviations

Books by the Author

1 Thess	*1 Thessalonians: A Commentary*, Crestwood, NY: St. Vladimir's Seminary Press, 1982
Gal	*Galatians: A Commentary*, Crestwood, NY: St. Vladimir's Seminary Press, 1994
OTI_1	*The Old Testament: An Introduction, Volume 1: Historical Traditions*, revised edition, Crestwood, NY: St. Vladimir's Seminary Press, 2003
OTI_2	*The Old Testament: An Introduction, Volume 2: Prophetic Traditions*, Crestwood, NY: St. Vladimir's Seminary Press, 1994
OTI_3	*The Old Testament: An Introduction, Volume 3: Psalms and Wisdom*, Crestwood, NY: St. Vladimir's Seminary Press, 1996
NTI_1	*The New Testament: An Introduction, Volume 1: Paul and Mark*, Crestwood, NY: St. Vladimir's Seminary Press, 1999
NTI_2	*The New Testament: An Introduction, Volume 2: Luke and Acts*, Crestwood, NY: St. Vladimir's Seminary Press, 2001
NTI_3	*The New Testament: An Introduction, Volume 3: Johannine Writings*, Crestwood, NY: St. Vladimir's Seminary Press, 2004
NTI_4	*The New Testament: An Introduction, Volume 4: Matthew and the Canon*, St. Paul, MN: OCABS Press, 2009
C-Gen	*Genesis: A Commentary*. The Chrysostom Bible. St. Paul, MN: OCABS Press, 2009
C-Phil	*Philippians: A Commentary*. The Chrysostom Bible. St. Paul, MN: OCABS Press, 2009
C-Rom	*Romans: A Commentary*. The Chrysostom Bible. St. Paul, MN: OCABS Press, 2010
LAC	*Land and Covenant*, St. Paul, MN: OCABS Press, 2009

Abbreviations

Books of the Old Testament*

Gen	Genesis	Job	Job	Hab	Habakkuk
Ex	Exodus	Ps	Psalms	Zeph	Zephaniah
Lev	Leviticus	Prov	Proverbs	Hag	Haggai
Num	Numbers	Eccl	Ecclesiastes	Zech	Zechariah
Deut	Deuteronomy	Song	Song of Solomon	Mal	Malachi
Josh	Joshua	Is	Isaiah	Tob	Tobit
Judg	Judges	Jer	Jeremiah	Jdt	Judith
Ruth	Ruth	Lam	Lamentations	Wis	Wisdom
1 Sam	1 Samuel	Ezek	Ezekiel	Sir	Sirach (Ecclesiasticus)
2 Sam	2 Samuel	Dan	Daniel	Bar	Baruch
1 Kg	1 Kings	Hos	Hosea	1 Esd	1 Esdras
2 Kg	2 Kings	Joel	Joel	2 Esd	2 Esdras
1 Chr	1 Chronicles	Am	Amos	1 Macc	1 Maccabees
2 Chr	2 Chronicles	Ob	Obadiah	2 Macc	2 Maccabees
Ezra	Ezra	Jon	Jonah	3 Macc	3 Maccabees
Neh	Nehemiah	Mic	Micah	4 Macc	4 Maccabees
Esth	Esther	Nah	Nahum		

Books of the New Testament

Mt	Matthew	Eph	Ephesians	Heb	Hebrews
Mk	Mark	Phil	Philippians	Jas	James
Lk	Luke	Col	Colossians	1 Pet	1 Peter
Jn	John	1 Thess	1 Thessalonians	2 Pet	2 Peter
Acts	Acts	2 Thess	2 Thessalonians	1 Jn	1 John
Rom	Romans	1 Tim	1 Timothy	2 Jn	2 John
1 Cor	1 Corinthians	2 Tim	2 Timothy	3 Jn	3 John
2 Cor	2 Corinthians	Titus	Titus	Jude	Jude
Gal	Galatians	Philem	Philemon	Rev	Revelation

*Following the larger canon known as the Septuagint.

Contents

Preface	*13*
Introduction	*19*

Part I - Colossians

Chapter 1	***23***
Vv. 1-2	*23*
Vv. 3-8	*26*
Vv. 9-23	*36*
Vv. 24-29	*54*
Chapter 2	***61***
Vv. 1-5	*61*
Vv. 6-15	*62*
Vv. 16-23	*70*
Chapter 3	***79***
Vv. 1-17	*79*
Vv. 18-25	*87*
V. 4:1	*87*
Chapter 4	***93***
Vv. 2-6	*93*
Vv. 7-18	*94*

Part II - Philemon

Chapter 5	***109***
Vv. 1-3	*109*
Vv. 4-7	*112*
Vv. 8-16	*117*

Vv. 17-20	*123*
Vv. 21-22	*125*
Vv. 23-25	*126*
Further Reading	***129***
Commentaries and Studies	*129*
Articles	*130*

Preface

The present Bible Commentary Series is not so much in honor of John Chrysostom as it is to continue and promote his legacy as an interpreter of the biblical texts for preaching and teaching God's congregation, in order to prod its members to proceed on the way they started when they accepted God's calling. Chrysostom's virtual uniqueness is that he did not subscribe to any hermeneutic or methodology, since this would amount to introducing an extra-textual authority over the biblical texts. For him, scripture is its own interpreter. Listening to the texts time and again allowed him to realize that "call" and "read (aloud)" are not interconnected realities; rather, they are one reality since they both are renditions of the same Hebrew verb *qara'*. Given that words read aloud are words of instruction for one "to do them," the only valid reaction would be to hear, listen, obey, and abide by these words. All these connotations are subsumed in the same Hebrew verb *šama'*. On the other hand, these scriptural "words of life" are presented as readily understandable utterances of a father to his children (Isaiah 1:2-3). The recipients are never asked to engage in an intellectual debate with their divine instructor, or even among themselves, to fathom what he is saying. The Apostle to the Gentiles followed in the footsteps of the Prophets to Israel by handing down to them the Gospel, that is, the Law of God's Spirit through his Christ (Romans 8:2; Galatians 6:2) as fatherly instruction (1 Corinthians 4:15). He in turn wrote readily understandable letters to be read aloud. It is in these same footsteps that Chrysostom followed, having learned from both the Prophets and Paul that the same "words of life" carry also the sentence of death at the hand of the scriptural God, Judge of all

(Deuteronomy 28; Joshua 8:32-35; Psalm 82; Matthew 3:4-12; Romans 2:12-16; 1 Corinthians 10:1-11; Revelation 20:11-15).

While theological debates and hermeneutical theories come and go after having fed their proponents and their fans with passing human glory, the Golden Mouth's expository homilies, through the centuries, fed and still feed myriads of believers in so many traditions and countries. Virtually banned from dogmatic treatises, he survives in the hearts of "those who have ears to hear." His success is due to his commitment to exegesis rather than to futile hermeneutics. The latter behaves as someone who dictates on a living organism what it is supposed to be, whereas exegesis submits to that organism and endeavors to decipher it through trial and error. There is as much a far cry between the text and the theories about it as there is between a living organism and the theories about it. The biblical texts are the reality of God imparted through their being read aloud in the midst of the congregation, disregarding the value of the sermon that follows. The sermon, much less a theological treatise, is at best an invitation to hear and obey the text. Assessing the shape of an invitation card has no value whatsoever when it comes to the dinner itself; the guests are fed by the dinner, not by the invitation or its phrasing (Luke 14:16-24; Matthew 22:1-14).

This commentary series does not intend to promote Chrysostom's ideas as a public relation manager would do, but rather to follow in the footsteps of his approach as true children and heirs are expected to do. He used all the contemporary tools at his disposal to communicate God's written instruction to his hearers, as a doctor would with his patients, without spending unnecessary energy on peripheral debates requiring the use of professional jargon incomprehensible to the commoner. The writers of this series will try to do the same: muster to the best of their ability all necessary contemporary knowledge to communicate to the general readers the biblical message without burdening them with data unnecessary for that purpose. Whenever it will be deemed necessary or even helpful to do so, and in order to curtail burdensome and lengthy technical asides within the commentaries, specialized monographs related either to specific topics or to the scriptural background—literary, sociopolitical, or archeological—will be issued as companions to the series.

Paul Nadim Tarazi
Editor

Introduction

What is striking about both Paul's Letter to the Colossians and his Letter to Philemon is that addressees named at the beginning of each letter are found exclusively in these two Pauline epistles and nowhere else in the New Testament. This is strange, to say the least, given that the Book of Acts gives details about the Apostle's visits to each of the churches to whom he wrote his letters. Even Galatia is mentioned in Acts (16:6; 18:23) and 1 Corinthians (16:1). Because of the correspondence of personal names occurring in Colossians and Philemon, many commentaries deal with both epistles in one volume. Further, one can safely conclude, as a great number of scholars do, that Philemon was a Roman patrician of Colossae.

The most probable explanation for Colossae is that it was intended metaphorically and thus chosen because of that name's connotation: the Colossus of Rhodes, built at the entrance of the harbor of that city in honor of Helios, the Sun deity. Given the expanse of the cult of Mithras—identified with Helios—who was heavily honored in Rome and throughout the empire especially among the soldiers, it would appear that Colossae is meant to be a stand-in for Rome itself.

Another indication of the link between Colossians and Romans is that, according to the New Testament data, these two epistles are addressed to churches Paul had not established nor had previous contacts with. The letter's extolling of Christ over and above any power, heavenly as well as earthly, corroborates this premise. In spite of God's Christ's having been crucified (Col 1:20) by the Roman authorities and of God's ambassador's being fettered (4:18) in a Roman jail, "He [God] disarmed the principalities and powers and made a public example of them, triumphing over them in him [Christ]" (2:15) and "To them [his saints] God chose to make known how great among the Gentiles are the riches of the glory of this mystery, which is Christ among you,[1] the hope of glory" (1:27).

As for the letter to Philemon, it is intended, as I shall make clear in my comments, to "fetter" a free Roman patrician of the "mighty" city of Colossae to the gospel whose main injunction is the love for the needy neighbor. In that sense, it is as metaphorical as Colossians and, thus, an example for every one of its hearers to emulate. In this sense, both Colossians and Philemon, when understood against their original background, are lessons for the ages.

In this commentary series, I have included both Greek and English texts for each verse. The English is the RSV translation, which I have been using in my writings. In my comments, however, I often defer to the Greek with my own translation in order to render the meaning as close as possible to the original text.

---

[1] RSV has "in you."

Part I

Colossians

Chapter 1

Vv. 1-2 ¹Παῦλος ἀπόστολος Χριστοῦ Ἰησοῦ διὰ θελήματος θεοῦ καὶ Τιμόθεος ὁ ἀδελφὸς ² τοῖς ἐν Κολοσσαῖς ἁγίοις καὶ πιστοῖς ἀδελφοῖς ἐν Χριστῷ, χάρις ὑμῖν καὶ εἰρήνη ἀπὸ θεοῦ πατρὸς ἡμῶν

¹Paul, an apostle of Christ Jesus by the will of God, and Timothy our brother, ²to the saints and faithful brethren in Christ at Colossae: Grace to you and peace from God our Father.

Paul begins this letter with his usual introduction identifying himself as an apostle of Christ Jesus. Timothy, his helper, is referred to as "brother." Paul alone, among the leaders of his churches, is the "apostle of the Messiah Jesus." Actually, according to the Jerusalem agreement, he is the sole apostle to the Gentiles, just as Peter is the sole apostle to the Jews of the diaspora (Gal 2:7-8). Furthermore, Paul's apostleship is not to be questioned since it originates by God's will (*thelēmatos*), which is a shortened formula (see also 1 Cor 1:1; 2 Cor 1:1; Eph 1:1) for the detailed "not from men nor through man, but through Jesus Christ and God the Father" (Gal 1:1). Moreover, God's will for the apostle can be neither explained nor challenged, since it is ultimately for a purpose, as we hear in the letter to the Galatians: "But when he [God] who had set me apart before I was born, and had called me through his grace, was pleased (*evdokēsen*) to reveal his Son to me, *in order that* I might preach him among the Gentiles" (vv.15-16). Indeed, earlier in that letter Paul used the term "will" in conjunction with the salvation bestowed to all: "Grace to you and peace from God the Father and our Lord Jesus Christ, who gave himself for our sins to deliver us from the present evil age, according to the will (*thelēma*) of our God and Father." (vv.3-4) In Ephesians, God's "will" and "pleasure" are joined in one action: "He destined us in love to be his sons through Jesus Christ, according to the (good) pleasure (*evdokian*) of his will (*thelēmatos*), to the praise of his glorious grace which he freely bestowed on us in the Beloved." (1:5-6).

Directly in Colossians 1:1 Paul couples himself with Timothy. In doing so, Paul is presenting Timothy as his heir apparent, just as he did in Philippians.[1] By being included in the greeting of the letter, Timothy is to function, after Paul's demise, as the representative of Christ himself who is "the first-born among many brethren" (Rom 8:29). Thus, Paul is leaving the care of the "saints" of Colossae to Timothy, who is to keep them "faithful" to God's will.

As God's plenipotentiary emissary for their salvation, Paul addresses the Colossians as his brethren, just as he refers to Timothy. The addressees are brethren who are called to be saints (*hagiois*; holy, Col 1:2). Indeed, just as the apostolate is a calling (Rom 1:1), so is holiness or sanctification (v.7; see also Rom 6:22 and 1 Thess 4:7). However, this is not to be misunderstood. Holiness is not something to be earned; rather it is a gift to be maintained, and it can be lost should the believers not abide by God's will: "Do you not know that the unrighteous will not inherit the kingdom of God? Do not be deceived; neither the immoral, nor idolaters, nor adulterers, nor sexual perverts, nor thieves, nor the greedy, nor drunkards, nor revilers, nor robbers will inherit the kingdom of God. And such were some of you. But you were washed, you were sanctified (*hēgiasthēte*; made holy), you were justified in the name of the Lord Jesus Christ and in the Spirit of our God." (1 Cor 6:9-11) How is one to maintain the gift of holiness? By remaining

---

[1] See my comments on Phil 1:1 and 2:19-24 in *C-Phil*.

faithful (*pistois*; trustworthy, Col 1:2) to the calling to abide by God's commandments: "Only, let every one lead the life which the Lord has assigned to him, and in which God has called him. This is my rule in all the churches. Was any one at the time of his call already circumcised? Let him not seek to remove the marks of circumcision. Was any one at the time of his call uncircumcised? Let him not seek circumcision. For neither circumcision counts for anything nor uncircumcision, but keeping the commandments of God." (1 Cor 7:17-19) Put otherwise, the Colossians maintain the holiness they were granted by trusting (having faith [*pistis*]) that the commands of God are for their own good. Hence the overarching appellation of Paul's followers as "faithful, trusting" (*pistevontes*) is with the hope that, when tested—a test that even Paul is not exempt from (4:1-5)—they will be found "trustworthy" (*pistoi*).

Paul wishes God's grace and peace on his hearers. Grace is point A of the path; it is through sheer graciousness on God's part to have bestowed his gift on the Colossians by including them among his "holy ones." And that happened through Paul's apostolic preaching. However, the second wish, the peace of the Kingdom, which is point Z of the same path, lies ahead and is out of Paul's hands. That is why it is a wish *on hope* (Rom 5:1-5). Indeed, at the end of the letter, after having guided the Colossians through instruction as to how to "stay the course," Paul can only leave them at point A (Grace be with you; Col 4:18c). They will attain the peace of God's kingdom only by following the instruction consigned in his letter. Thus, in this sense, he cannot do more than Moses did in Deuteronomy: bid farewell to the people and then die, leaving them with his instructions contained in the Book of Deuteronomy.

Vv. 3-8 ³ Εὐχαριστοῦμεν τῷ θεῷ πατρὶ τοῦ κυρίου ἡμῶν Ἰησοῦ Χριστοῦ πάντοτε περὶ ὑμῶν προσευχόμενοι, ⁴ ἀκούσαντες τὴν πίστιν ὑμῶν ἐν Χριστῷ Ἰησοῦ καὶ τὴν ἀγάπην ἣν ἔχετε εἰς πάντας τοὺς ἁγίους ⁵ διὰ τὴν ἐλπίδα τὴν ἀποκειμένην ὑμῖν ἐν τοῖς οὐρανοῖς, ἣν προηκούσατε ἐν τῷ λόγῳ τῆς ἀληθείας τοῦ εὐαγγελίου ⁶ τοῦ παρόντος εἰς ὑμᾶς, καθὼς καὶ ἐν παντὶ τῷ κόσμῳ ἐστὶν καρποφορούμενον καὶ αὐξανόμενον καθὼς καὶ ἐν ὑμῖν, ἀφ᾽ ἧς ἡμέρας ἠκούσατε καὶ ἐπέγνωτε τὴν χάριν τοῦ θεοῦ ἐν ἀληθείᾳ· ⁷ καθὼς ἐμάθετε ἀπὸ Ἐπαφρᾶ τοῦ ἀγαπητοῦ συνδούλου ἡμῶν, ὅς ἐστιν πιστὸς ὑπὲρ ὑμῶν διάκονος τοῦ Χριστοῦ, ⁸ ὁ καὶ δηλώσας ἡμῖν τὴν ὑμῶν ἀγάπην ἐν πνεύματι.

³*We always thank God, the Father of our Lord Jesus Christ, when we pray for you,* ⁴ *because we have heard of your faith in Christ Jesus and of the love which you have for all the saints,* ⁵*because of the hope laid up for you in heaven. Of this you have heard before in the word of the truth, the gospel* ⁶*which has come to you, as indeed in the whole world it is bearing fruit and growing—so among yourselves, from the day you heard and understood the grace of God in truth,* ⁷ *as you learned it from Epaphras our beloved fellow servant. He is a faithful minister of Christ on our behalf* ⁸*and has made known to us your love in the Spirit.*

Since Paul, as apostle, is the high priest of the Jerusalem above, he starts by thanking God on behalf of his flock.[2] If God is the father of the "brethren" (Col 1:2), it is because he is the father of the Messiah Jesus, the "firstborn." The Messiah, as king, is by definition "Son of God" (Ps 2:6-7), and as king is, ex officio, the high priest. This is clear from the story of the dedication of the temple when Solomon prays on behalf of the people (1 Kg 8:22-61). And since the king has to tend to the socio-political affairs of the kingdom, he assigns at will one of the temple priests to be the high priest in his stead (2:26-27; 4:2). In this sense, as the

---

[2] See my comments in *C-Rom* 227-8.

high priest, Paul is actually the locum tenens of the one king and high priest, Jesus Christ.[3] Paul is Christ's "sent" (apostle; Col 1:1), his "co-worker" (1 Cor 3:9).

Just as he does in 1 Thessalonians 1:3, Paul here remembers in his prayer the faith, love, and hope of his addressees. As will become clear from the rest of Colossians 1, this sequence is causal as well as chronological: first faith, then love, and finally hope. Faith is actually the trust one puts in the gospel teaching which is a law, a set of commands that are summed up in the love for the neighbor (Rom 13:8-10; Gal 5:13-15; see also Mt 22:34-40/Mk 12:28-34/Lk 10:25-37). Indeed, the trust is "in the Messiah Jesus" (Col 1:4a), that is, in his teaching, which Paul refers to as "the law of the Messiah" (Gal 6:2). The object of the love is "all the saints" (Col 1:4b). It is thus love for the others in the community which is the sign as to whether or not one has trusted in the gospel message, as Paul masterfully puts it elsewhere: "For in Christ Jesus neither circumcision nor uncircumcision is of any avail, but faith working through love." (Gal 5:6) By comparing this statement with its parallel in 1 Corinthians quoted earlier (For neither circumcision counts for anything nor uncircumcision, but keeping the commandments of God; 7:19), one sees again that indeed the gospel is tantamount to God's law, his directive, for us to love indiscriminately everyone who needs care.

However, this is not the end of the story since righteousness guaranteed through faith (Gal 2:16; see also Rom 5:1) is actually a verdict issued by the divine court: only God can declare us righteous. Such declaration will not take place until judgment day (1 Cor 4:1-5). This explains why "by faith, *we wait for*

---

[3] This theme is developed in Hebrews.

(*apekdekhometha*) the hope of righteousness" (Gal 5:5; see also Rom 8:25). That the final verdict is still ahead of us can be seen in that the verb "wait for" is found elsewhere only in relation to God's final intervention (Rom 8:19, 23, 25; 1 Cor 1:7; Phil 3:20; Heb 9:28; 1 Pet 3:20). That is why both our trust in Christ's teaching to love the others and this same love for the others are *dia* (because of, in view of, for the sake of) the hope "laid up in the heavens" (Col 1:5a) "whence we await (*apekdekhometha*) a Savior, the Lord Jesus Christ" (Phil 3:20). This hope was conveyed to the Colossians in "the word of the truth of the gospel" (Col 1:5b).

The redundant accumulation of nouns referring to the same matter is a trademark of Colossians and its counterpart, Ephesians. Since the texts were written to be heard, such literary devices were used to impress the hearer. The phrase "the word of the truth of the gospel" is actually a stacking of three words that mean "the gospel message *indeed*." This is corroborated by the parallel statement in Ephesians 1:13 that reads "the word of truth, the gospel of (leading to) your salvation," where the phrase "word of truth" is clearly another way to say "gospel." Both statements hark back to Galatians where we hear twice "the truth of the gospel" (2:5, 14) and once simply "the truth" (5:7). Thus, all three terms, "word," "truth," and "gospel," point to the one and same reality: Paul's preaching. The piling up of the three words together with the preceding "you previously heard" and the following "which has come to you" is intended to underscore that the message consigned in writing in this letter had *indeed* been conveyed by Paul to the Colossians, a fact that cannot be denied. The reason for such aural "bombardment" is to put pressure on the hearers. What had been previously said is now consigned as scripture for the ages. The Colossians and their progeny are bound to hear it time and again until the Lord's coming. This intention of the repetition is actually underscored in one of the closing remarks of this letter: "And when this letter has been read among you, have it read also in the church of the Laodiceans; and see that you read also the letter from Laodicea."[4] (4:16) Not only are the Colossians to hear what Paul wrote to them, but also what he wrote to at least another church, which cannot be but the same message as pointed out many times by Paul himself: "Therefore I sent to you Timothy, my beloved and faithful child in the Lord, to remind you of my ways in Christ, as I teach them everywhere in every church" (1 Cor 4:17); "This is my rule in all the churches" (7:17b); "Now concerning the contribution for the saints: as I directed the churches of Galatia, so you also are to do." (16:1)

The gospel word "came" to the Colossians, which is the translation of the Greek verb *pareimi*. This verb actually means "be present" and is of the same root as the noun *parousia* (presence, coming [as in becoming present]). Usually, to speak of being present, Paul uses either the plain verb *pareimi* (1 Cor 5:3; 2 Cor 10:2, 11; 13:2, 10) or the verb followed by *pros hymas* (toward [among] you; 2 Cor 11:9; Gal 4:18, 20). In Colossians 1:6 we have the sole instance of the verb *pareimi* followed by *eis hymas* (to, unto you) which reflects a movement toward something. Such is confirmed in that, in the other instances where reference is not to Paul's presence or absence, but rather to his apostolic activity, we encounter profusely the verb *erkhomai* (come, arrive). The unique use of *pareimi* (be present) followed by *eis* (to) here reflects Paul's understanding, developed

---

[4] The Greek verb *anaginōskō* used thrice in this verse means "read aloud" and not with the eyes as we understand "reading" nowadays. Notice how RSV is forced to add "aloud" in translating Rev 1:3 "Blessed is he who reads aloud (*ho anaginōskōn*; in the singular) the words of the prophecy, and blessed are those who hear (*hoi akouontes*; in the plural), and who keep what is written therein; for the time is near."

in all his letters, that the real and full presence of the Lord Jesus Christ lies in the "words" themselves of the gospel preaching (Col 1:5). And if so, then the gospel brings not only salvation but also and at the same time the judgment entailed in the Lord's *parousia*. Put otherwise, the *lordly* "presence" of Jesus Christ is always in "power"—power to save and power to judge. It is similar to that of God in the Pentateuch where he saves Israel out of Egypt and brings them into the wilderness where he delivers to them his "words" unto judgment, that is to say, unto curse as well as blessing (Lev 26 and Deut 28). It is only insofar as we implement the divine will to love our fellow man that we hope to reach the peace of the Kingdom.

In order to give support to the Colossians in their endeavor Paul tells them that the gospel is actually being preached in the entire world, that is to say, throughout the Roman empire, and it is actually "bearing fruit and growing" (Col 1:6). The use of this sequence is striking and is obviously intentional since it is repeated in v.10. Instead of the more natural sequence "growing and bearing fruit," the phrase actually means "bearing fruit and (still) growing (to bear more fruit)." Thus whatever fruit is borne is no indication of the full growth, which is in the hands of God (2:19), who alone "gives the growth" (1 Cor 3:6-7). The end will be reached according to God's will and Colossae, in spite of its "colossal" status, is not the "end of the world," just part of it (Col 1:6a). This is clearly intended to allude that Rome, at least for Paul, is not the center of the world, but merely a stop on his way to Spain (Rom 15:25, 28).

On the other hand, the combination of "bearing fruit" (*karpophoroumenon*) and "growing" (*avxanomenon*), unique in the New Testament, seems to suggest a new creation, given that in Genesis 1 we repeatedly hear words from these two roots:

And God said, "Let the earth put forth vegetation, plants yielding seed, and fruit trees (*xylon karpimon*) bearing fruit (*poioun karpon*) in which is their seed, each according to its kind, upon the earth." And it was so. The earth brought forth vegetation, plants yielding seed according to their own kinds, and fruit trees (*xylon karpimon*) bearing fruit (*poioun karpon*) in which is their seed, each according to its kind. And God saw that it was good ... And God blessed them, saying, "Be fruitful (*avxanesthe*) and multiply and fill (*plērōsate*) the waters in the seas, and let birds multiply on the earth." And God blessed them, and God said to them, "Be fruitful (*avxanesthe*) and multiply, and fill (*plērōsate*) the earth and subdue it; and have dominion over the fish of the sea and over the birds of the air and over every living thing that moves upon the earth." (vv.11-12, 22, 28)

The connection is even more evident when one takes into consideration the high incidence of the root *plērō*— indicating "fullness" in Colossians, nine times in four chapters.[5]

Through the gospel preached by Paul, God is guiding the entire Roman empire to the fullness it is dreaming of—the peace, the *pax Romana*. However, that peace is not secured by the sword of the Roman emperor, but with the shed blood of God's messiah (Col 1:20). The Colossians are to realize that, in spite of what appears as a "weak" instrument when compared to the "mighty" sword, the seed of the peace of the Kingdom has been sown and its growth is unstoppable:

> The kingdom of God is as if a man should throw seed upon the ground, and should sleep and rise night and day, and the seed should sprout and grow, he knows not how. The earth produces (*karpophorei*) of itself (automatically; *avtomatē*), first the blade, then the ear, then the full (*plērē*) grain in the ear. But when the

---

[5] Col 1:9, 19, 24, 25; 2:2, 9, 10; 4:12, 17.

fruit (*karpos*) is ripe, at once he puts in the sickle, because the harvest has come. (Mk 4:26-29)[6]

Just as the growth is directly linked to the seed that is sown freely and abundantly (Mk 4:3-8), so the path to the peace of the Kingdom began on the day the Colossians heard "the word of truth" and acknowledged that it was "in truth" the expression of God's sheer grace toward them (Col 1:6b).[7]

As he does in his parallel letter to the Philippians,[8] Paul leaves his addressees in the care of a certain Epaphras, the shortened form of Epahroditus found in Philippians. In Philippians Paul mentions Epaphroditus twice, once early on (Phil 2:25) and once in the closing remarks (4:18); here also we hear of Epaphras once at the beginning of the letter (Col 1:7) and another time at the end (4:12). As I explained in my commentary on Philippians, that name is intentionally symbolic, as are the majority, if not all, of the names in the New Testament. The Greek *epaphroditos*[9] is an adjective meaning "filled with pleasure (blessing, fortune)," and thus "bestowing pleasure (blessing, fortune)." Its counterpart in Latin is *felix* (felicitous, fortunate, blessed). Thus Epaphras is the consummate "fortunate" someone

---

[6] This parable is unique to Mark and its terminology corresponds closely to that of Col 1:6-10. In my *NTI₁* I have defended the thesis that Colossians functioned as the charter of the Pauline school and that Mark was written in conjunction with it, with both works "dipping into" Galatians.

[7] See also 1 Thess 2:13 (And we also thank God constantly for this, that when you received the *word* of God which you heard from us, you accepted it not as the *word* of men but as what it *truly* (*alēthōs*) is, the *word* of God, which is at work in you believers).

[8] Both Philippians and Colossians are the only letters not addressed to capitals of provinces. Philippi and Colossae function as mini-Romes as I explain in my Introductions to these epistles that bear thus close similarities in their compositions. See also the part on the Canon in my *NTI₄*.

[9] The Greek root is the name Aphrodite, the goddess of love and felicity.

who is blessed by God in order to bestow those blessings, in turn, on the Colossians. Epaphroditus functions in the same way in Philippians. Consequently both these names are to be taken in the sense that, besides Timothy, the outsider and Paul's plenipotentiary emissary, God will raise, according to his good pleasure, from among the addressed community the needed adjutants to help Timothy. Indeed Epaphroditus is introduced as a Philippian (Phil 2:25; 4:18) and Epaphras is introduced as a Colossian (4:12).

The symbolism of these two names is actually corroborated in the functional phraseology connected with each in the two letters.[10] In Philippians, Timothy is introduced on a par with Paul (1:1) and is singled out as his heir apparent (2:19-24) and Epaphroditus appears as third in line (vv.25-30), so to speak. Here in Colossians, Timothy is introduced merely as a brother, compared to Paul the apostle (1:1), and he is not mentioned again in the letter; it as though he is already "in the past." On the other hand, Epaphras is introduced early on in the letter (1:7-8) and again at the end (4:12), so that his mention brackets the letter as an *inclusio*. In other words, in Colossians, Epaphras is presented as de facto second in line to Paul, in lieu of Timothy. Indeed, he is put on a par with Paul as his co-slave (*syndoulou*) and, more importantly, as "deacon" (*diakonos*) (1:7), which is the main function of Paul as apostle in Colossians (1:23, 25). Furthermore, Epaphras is a "faithful" deacon (1:7), thus a worthy leader of the "faithful" Colossians (1:2). Finally, whereas Timothy is the one who reports of the love of the Thessalonians to Paul (1 Thess 3:6), in Colossians it is Epaphras who fulfills this duty (Col 1:8). It is he, instead of Timothy, who is the "link" between Paul and the Colossians. So, in his own

---

[10] I discussed in detail Epaphroditus in *C-Phil* 143-7.

way, Paul is preparing the Colossians for the time when not only he but also Timothy will be gone and Epaphras will be the "teacher" (1:7) in Paul's stead. And as in Ephesians (4:20) and in Philippians (4:9) the addressees are told it is from the teacher that "you learned" (*emathete*).

In Philippians the singling out of "bishops and deacons" among the addressees reflected the setting of table fellowship in the Pauline house churches, during which fellowship at the *one* table took place the imparting of the *one* gospel teaching. The centrality of the household table fellowship in Colossians is corroborated by the high incidence of the root *khar*— whence both "grace, gracefulness" (*kharis*) and "thanksgiving (*evkharistia* [Eucharist]; recognition of the gracefulness)": no less than fourteen times in four chapters.[11] This stress on table fellowship is actually a staple of Colossians. Not only Paul and Epaphras are "deacons (table ministers)," but so also are Tychicus (4:7; *diakonos*) and Archippus (v.17; *diakonian* [ministry]), which is a feature unique to Colossians. The choice of names for the deacons betrays the importance of table fellowship in the author's mind. Just as Epaphras means "anyone chosen through fortuity," so does Tychicus (*Tykhikos*) since the Greek *tykhē* means "fate, chance, fortuity." Archippus (*Arkhippos*) means "master of the horse, owner of horses" and thus a rich and powerful person. The intention is clear. The first two names are a reminder that anyone chosen by God to be a "table minister" is to be respected as a "teacher." On the other hand, although in a Roman household the position of "table minister" is assigned to slaves, when a Roman household becomes a (house) church of God, it is an honor even for the rich and powerful members, as

---

[11] 1:2, 3, 6, 12; 2:7, 13; 3:13 (twice), 15, 16, 17; 4:2, 6, 18.

evident in the name Archippus, to hold the office of "table minister."[12] Even Paul himself is such a minister.[13]

The ministry is essentially one of teaching, as is clear from Colossians 1:7: "as you *learned* from Epaphras our beloved fellow slave (*syndoulou*) who is a faithful minister (*diakonos*) of Christ on our behalf.[14]" Still, this "teaching ministry" of the "table slave" is one of example as to how to love the others. That is why Epaphras is said here to have reported to Paul only the love displayed by the Colossians (1:8) compared to Timothy's report that included both the faith and love of the Thessalonians (1 Thess 3:6). This does not mean that love is a lesser matter since it is actually the test that validates the trust in the teaching (Gal 5:6). Rather, the express duty of a deacon is to keep an eye on the brotherly love that is mainly revealed at table fellowship. Actually, Epaphras is said to be "faithful" (*pistos*; Col 1:7) and, as such, he can be a leading example as well as a teacher to the Colossians who are supposed to be "faithful" (v.2).

The importance of this diaconal function is best seen in the story of the assignment of the seven deacons; their specific duties allowed the apostles to be free to preach the word (Acts 6:1-7). The importance, if not centrality, of the diaconal function can further be seen in the lengthy accounts of the subsequent activity of the first two deacons, Stephen and Philip. The first preached the gospel to the Jews and was martyred for its sake (7:8-60); the second was the first to preach the same gospel to Samaritans and

---

[12] Compare with the Lord's sayings regarding table ministry as the office of the "great" (Mt 20:25-28; 23:11-12; 9:35; 10:42-45; Lk 22:26-27).

[13] "Table minister" in Colossians has the same function as "slave" in Philippians. In either instance Paul is requesting his hearers to follow in his footsteps: be a servant unto others, as he originally taught in Galatians (5:13).

[14] Some manuscripts have "for your sake" (*hyper hymōn*) instead of "on our behalf" (*hyper hēmōn*). The result, nevertheless, is the same.

far away Gentiles (8:4-40). The close relation between preaching the gospel, including the trust in it, on the one hand, and living it at table fellowship, on the other hand, is borne out in Galatians 2:1-14 (see also 1 Corinthians 11:17-33 and Romans 14:1-15:6).

Vv. 9-23 ⁹ Διὰ τοῦτο καὶ ἡμεῖς, ἀφ' ἧς ἡμέρας ἠκούσαμεν, οὐ παυόμεθα ὑπὲρ ὑμῶν προσευχόμενοι καὶ αἰτούμενοι, ἵνα πληρωθῆτε τὴν ἐπίγνωσιν τοῦ θελήματος αὐτοῦ ἐν πάσῃ σοφίᾳ καὶ συνέσει πνευματικῇ, ¹⁰ περιπατῆσαι ἀξίως τοῦ κυρίου εἰς πᾶσαν ἀρεσκείαν, ἐν παντὶ ἔργῳ ἀγαθῷ καρποφοροῦντες καὶ αὐξανόμενοι τῇ ἐπιγνώσει τοῦ θεοῦ, ¹¹ ἐν πάσῃ δυνάμει δυναμούμενοι κατὰ τὸ κράτος τῆς δόξης αὐτοῦ εἰς πᾶσαν ὑπομονὴν καὶ μακροθυμίαν. Μετὰ χαρᾶς ¹² εὐχαριστοῦντες τῷ πατρὶ τῷ ἱκανώσαντι ὑμᾶς εἰς τὴν μερίδα τοῦ κλήρου τῶν ἁγίων ἐν τῷ φωτί· ¹³ ὃς ἐρρύσατο ἡμᾶς ἐκ τῆς ἐξουσίας τοῦ σκότους καὶ μετέστησεν εἰς τὴν βασιλείαν τοῦ υἱοῦ τῆς ἀγάπης αὐτοῦ, ¹⁴ ἐν ᾧ ἔχομεν τὴν ἀπολύτρωσιν, τὴν ἄφεσιν τῶν ἁμαρτιῶν· ¹⁵ ὅς ἐστιν εἰκὼν τοῦ θεοῦ τοῦ ἀοράτου, πρωτότοκος πάσης κτίσεως, ¹⁶ ὅτι ἐν αὐτῷ ἐκτίσθη τὰ πάντα ἐν τοῖς οὐρανοῖς καὶ ἐπὶ τῆς γῆς, τὰ ὁρατὰ καὶ τὰ ἀόρατα, εἴτε θρόνοι εἴτε κυριότητες εἴτε ἀρχαὶ εἴτε ἐξουσίαι· τὰ πάντα δι' αὐτοῦ καὶ εἰς αὐτὸν ἔκτισται· ¹⁷ καὶ αὐτός ἐστιν πρὸ πάντων καὶ τὰ πάντα ἐν αὐτῷ συνέστηκεν, ¹⁸ καὶ αὐτός ἐστιν ἡ κεφαλὴ τοῦ σώματος τῆς ἐκκλησίας· ὅς ἐστιν ἀρχή, πρωτότοκος ἐκ τῶν νεκρῶν, ἵνα γένηται ἐν πᾶσιν αὐτὸς πρωτεύων, ¹⁹ ὅτι ἐν αὐτῷ εὐδόκησεν πᾶν τὸ πλήρωμα κατοικῆσαι ²⁰ καὶ δι' αὐτοῦ ἀποκαταλλάξαι τὰ πάντα εἰς αὐτόν, εἰρηνοποιήσας διὰ τοῦ αἵματος τοῦ σταυροῦ αὐτοῦ, [δι' αὐτοῦ] εἴτε τὰ ἐπὶ τῆς γῆς εἴτε τὰ ἐν τοῖς οὐρανοῖς. ²¹ Καὶ ὑμᾶς ποτε ὄντας ἀπηλλοτριωμένους καὶ ἐχθροὺς τῇ διανοίᾳ ἐν τοῖς ἔργοις τοῖς πονηροῖς, ²² νυνὶ δὲ ἀποκατήλλαξεν ἐν τῷ σώματι τῆς σαρκὸς αὐτοῦ διὰ τοῦ θανάτου παραστῆσαι ὑμᾶς ἁγίους καὶ ἀμώμους καὶ ἀνεγκλήτους κατενώπιον αὐτοῦ, ²³ εἴ γε ἐπιμένετε τῇ πίστει τεθεμελιωμένοι καὶ ἑδραῖοι καὶ μὴ μετακινούμενοι ἀπὸ τῆς ἐλπίδος τοῦ εὐαγγελίου οὗ ἠκούσατε, τοῦ κηρυχθέντος ἐν

Chapter 1 ... 37

πάσῃ κτίσει τῇ ὑπὸ τὸν οὐρανόν, οὗ ἐγενόμην ἐγὼ Παῦλος διάκονος.

> *⁹And so, from the day we heard of it, we have not ceased to pray for you, asking that you may be filled with the knowledge of his will in all spiritual wisdom and understanding, ¹⁰ to lead a life worthy of the Lord, fully pleasing to him, bearing fruit in every good work and increasing in the knowledge of God. ¹¹May you be strengthened with all power, according to his glorious might, for all endurance and patience with joy, ¹² giving thanks to the Father, who has qualified us to share in the inheritance of the saints in light. ¹³ He has delivered us from the dominion of darkness and transferred us to the kingdom of his beloved Son, ¹⁴ in whom we have redemption, the forgiveness of sins. ¹⁵ He is the image of the invisible God, the first-born of all creation; ¹⁶ for in him all things were created, in heaven and on earth, visible and invisible, whether thrones or dominions or principalities or authorities—all things were created through him and for him. ¹⁷He is before all things, and in him all things hold together. ¹⁸He is the head of the body, the church; he is the beginning, the first-born from the dead, that in everything he might be pre-eminent. ¹⁹For in him all the fulness of God was pleased to dwell, ²⁰ and through him to reconcile to himself all things, whether on earth or in heaven, making peace by the blood of his cross. ²¹And you, who once were estranged and hostile in mind, doing evil deeds, ²²he has now reconciled in his body of flesh by his death, in order to present you holy and blameless and irreproachable before him, ²³provided that you continue in the faith, stable and steadfast, not shifting from the hope of the gospel which you heard, which has been preached to every creature under heaven, and of which I, Paul, became a minister.*

In Philippians, along with Christ, Paul gave himself, Timothy, and Epaphroditus as examples of behavior to be followed by the addressees.[15] The intention was to put pressure on his hearers. Here, in Colossians, he does the same. He begins with Epaphras,

---

[15] See *C-Phil* 104, 144-6.

moves to Christ (1:9-23), and ends with himself (1:24-2:5), then concludes with an exhortation for the Colossians to "walk" accordingly (v.6). Although, in this letter, Timothy is not singled out with a special passage as he was in Philippians (2:19-24), he nevertheless functions as an example to follow. Indeed, the appellation of "faithful brethren" (v.2) that Paul gives to the Colossians is split evenly between Timothy the "brother" (v.1) and Epaphras the "faithful" deacon (v.9). Actually, Timothy is the more encompassing example since "brother/brethren" is the classic common denominator of all the believers in the gospel,[16] whereas Epaphras is said to be faithful in his office as a deacon.

As in Philippians (2:6-11), the ultimate example to emulate is Christ, who is presented as an antitype of Caesar (Col 1:13-20). Here, however, before getting to Christ, Paul speaks of the gospel he preached to the Colossians. The reason is twofold. On the one hand, it allows him to introduce himself as an example of behavior for the Colossians (vv.24-29). On the other hand, and more importantly for the Colossians, as in the case of the Philippians and of all those whom Paul evangelized, the real and true Jesus Christ lies within the words Paul used to communicate his gospel. No one among the addressees of the Pauline letters has ever encountered "Christ in (according to) the flesh (*kata sarka*)" (2 Cor 5:16). For Paul's hearers, Jesus Christ is never a reality outside the gospel "word(s)." Therefore, Paul can logically[17] write later in the same letter: "For if some one comes and preaches *another Jesus* than the one we preached, or if you receive a different spirit from the one you received, or if you

---

[16] Although "faithful" is the other common title, however the Greek in that case is the present participle *pisteuōn/pisteuontes* and not the adjective *pistos/pistoi* which is used here of both the Colossians (v.1) and Epaphras (v.8)

[17] The pun is intended since "logically" is actually "logic-ally" (*logikōs*), that is to say, "in words," "according to the words used to communicate the point of the message."

accept a different gospel from the one you accepted, you submit to it readily enough." (11:4)

Consequently, for the hearers, the reality of Jesus Christ began on the "day" they received the gospel message (Phil 1:5). Still the "day" that ultimately matters is the "day of Christ" when accounting will be held as to whether the seed of that gospel will have borne the required fruit (vv.10-11). This is so central to Paul's mind that he repeats in Colossians 1:8-9 what he said in vv.3-4: the news of the Colossians' behavior, especially the expression of love for others (vv.4 and 8), is the reason for his thanksgiving to God (v.3) and his hope is that they continue in their efforts in this regard (vv.9-11). Notice how after having said earlier "when we pray (*prosevkhomenoi*) for you" (v.3), he insists "we *do not cease* (*ou pavometha*) to pray (*prosevkhomenoi*) for you and to request (from you; *aitoumenoi*)" (v.9a) that you may continue walking on this path (*peripatēsai*) (v.10). To be able to continue on that path, the Colossians are to be filled with the knowledge of the gospel Paul preached to them. This gospel is not "mental" knowledge of God, as matters unfortunately developed in classical theology. Rather the object as well as subject of such knowledge is the "will of God" (v.9b). And that will is expressed in the Law that we are to abide by: "But if you call yourself a Jew and rely *upon the law* and boast in God and know *the will* (*to thelēma*) and approve what is excellent, *because you are instructed in the law*." (Rom 2:17-18) That is why, later in the same letter, Paul insists that "the law is holy, and the commandment is holy and just and good" (7:12), and elsewhere that, although "neither circumcision counts for anything nor uncircumcision," however what actually counts is "keeping the commandments of God" (1 Cor 7:19). And since this Law is subsumed in the love for the neighbor (Rom 13:8-10; Gal 5:13-15), Paul's concern regarding this matter, which Epaphras has the mission to carry on after Paul's demise, brackets as an *inclusio* the entire letter to the Colossians:

> Of this you have heard before in the word of the truth, the gospel which has come to you, as indeed in the whole world it is bearing fruit and growing—so among yourselves, from the day you heard and understood the grace of God in truth, as you learned it from Epaphras our beloved fellow servant. He is a faithful minister of Christ on our behalf and has made known to us your love in the Spirit. And so, from the day we heard of it, we have not ceased to *pray* for you, asking that you may be filled (*plērōthēte*)[18] with the knowledge of *his will* in all spiritual wisdom and understanding (1:5b-9)

> Epaphras, who is one of yourselves, a servant of Christ Jesus, greets you, always remembering you earnestly in his *prayers*, that you may stand mature and fully assured (*peplērophorēmenoi*)[19] in all *the will of God.* (4:12)

Still, if the Colossians abide by God's will to love the others, thanksgiving is not due to them but to God (1:3-4) since, whatever they do in terms of "good work," they ultimately do "unto every good pleasure" (*eis pasan areskeian*) of God (v.10)[20] who "is at work in you, both to will and to work for his good pleasure (*hyper tēs evdokias*)" (Phil 2:13).[21] Indeed, without the communication of God's will to them, the Colossians would not have known what his will was all about in the first place. And the decision to communicate this information to them lay in God's will to do so since, after all, "Paul" is "an apostle of Christ

---

[18] From the root *plēro*—.
[19] Also from the root *plēro*—.
[20] RSV has "fully pleasing to him."
[21] *areskeia* and *evdokia* have the same connotation. The first bespeaks the action of the one who behaves to please someone else, and the second describes the attitude of the one who is pleased by the behavior of another.

Jesus by *the will of God*" (Col 1:1).[22] The close link between Colossians 1:1; 1:5b-9; and 4:12 is evident in the occurrences of divine "will" (*thelēma*) that, in the letter, are confined to these three instances. Moreover, the only other instance of God's "willing" something is found in 1:27 where the subject matter is the gospel preached by Paul:

> Now I rejoice in my sufferings for your sake, and in my flesh I complete what is lacking in Christ's afflictions for the sake of his body, that is, the church, of which I became a minister (*diakonos*) according to the divine office which was given to me for you, to fulfill (my mission regarding) *the word of God*, the mystery hidden for ages and generations but now made manifest to his saints. To them God *willed* (*ēthelēsen*) to make known how great among the Gentiles are the riches of the glory of this mystery, which is Christ in you, the hope of glory. (1:24-27)

Consequently, "the knowledge of God" in which the Colossians are to keep "bearing fruit and increasing" (v.10) is none other than "the knowledge of his will" (v.9), which is communicated to them through the gospel preached by Paul (v.5). That is why Paul can speak of the gospel itself as "bearing fruit and growing among yourselves" as well as "in the whole world" (v.6). And since the gospel is the command of God to love the others, it is ultimately "in all good work" that one is to walk and to continue bearing fruit and growing" (v.10).[23] I used "keep" and "continue" before "bearing fruit and growing," not

---

[22] We find the parallelism between God's "good pleasure" and "will" in Galatians. First we hear of God's will (*thelēma*; 1:4) in choosing Paul to be his apostle (v.1) and then of God's implementation of that will as "good pleasure" (*evdokēsen*; [God] was pleased) in vv.15-16.

[23] Notice how, in the original Greek, it is the phrase "in all good work" (*en panti ergō agathō*) that qualifies the subsequent participles "bearing fruit and growing" (*karpophorountes kai avxomenoi*) as well as the preceding infinitive "walk" (*peripatēsai*).

only because these two verbs are in the present participle in both verses 6 and 10, but also because of their sequence. Growing comes after planting and watering (1 Cor 3:6) with the ultimate purpose being the bearing of fruit, which is the basis for the divine judgment.[24] By mentioning twice "bearing fruit" before "growing," Paul is underscoring that the road to be walked by the believers never ends until the Lord comes and not when they feel they could cry "mission accomplished." Indeed, in Philippians, a parallel letter to Colossians, Paul writes: "Brethren, I do not consider that I have made it my own; but one thing I do, forgetting what lies behind and straining forward to what lies ahead, I press on toward the goal for the prize of the upward call of God in Christ Jesus." (Phil 3:13-14)

Again, all is divine grace. The Colossians are able to do their duty because they are "strengthened (*dynamoumenoi*; empowered) with all power (*dynamei*), according to the might of (that emanates from) his (divine) glory" (Col 1:11a). As for the Colossians' part, it consists in proceeding on the path "in all endurance and patience" yet "with joy" (v.11b) in spite of the sufferings and tribulations they have to endure (1 Thess 1:6; see also 3:1-4 and Rom 5:1-5). Furthermore, just as Paul does (Col 1:3), they are to offer thanks to God the Father who not only sustains them by empowering them to do his will, but actually initiated the whole process of making them fit (worthy, competent; *hikanōsanti*) to be part of the community of his saints (v.12). And as always, everything that God puts in motion for the good of the Gentile Colossians, he does through the intermediacy of Paul, the apostle to the Gentiles. In 2 Corinthians Paul states: "Such is the confidence that we have through Christ toward God. Not that we are competent

---

[24] Mt 3:10; 7:17-20; 12:33-37; 21:19; Lk 3:9; 6:43-45; 13:6-9.

(*hikanoi*) of ourselves to claim anything as coming from us; our competence (*hikanotēs*) is from God, who has made us competent (*hikanōsen*)[25] to be ministers (*diakonoi*) of a new covenant." (3:4-6a) In turn, the "minister (deacon) Paul" assigns Epaphras to that same ministry (Col 1:8). Thus, Paul is putting pressure on the Colossians by reminding them of the mechanism God set in motion, a mechanism requiring an entire chain of servants in order to secure that the Colossians end up *and remain* in the company of his saints. In order to walk this path, the Colossians need the light of the gospel teaching (v.12) which they originally did not have, thus being in the darkness and, consequently, wandering to and fro without being able to reach God's kingdom. They needed to be rescued from the oppressive dominion of that darkness in order to attain the Kingdom (v.13). Yet, rather than using the word "attain," they are said to be "transferred, translated" (*metestēsen*) into that Kingdom since all that happens to them actually happens *for* them: it originates in God's love for them (v.13b), and no one and nothing can possibly "separate us from the love of God in Christ Jesus our Lord" (Rom 8:39b). As Isaiah explained (Is 53), it is through Christ, that the Colossians, actually all of us, are granted redemption, that is to say, the forgiveness of sins (Col 1:14). Indeed, God's lamb in Isaiah is none other than his servant whose redemptive mission encompasses Israel and the nations alike (Is 42:6; 49:6).

As he does in Philippians 2:6-11, Paul uses the terminology describing the Isaianic servant of the Lord to portray the mission of Jesus Christ (Col 1:15-20). However, instead of bringing to the fore the difference between the disobedience of Adam and

---

[25] Besides Colossians, this is the only other instance of the verb *hikanoō* in the New Testament.

the obedience of the Lord's servant as he does in Philippians,[26] here in Colossians Paul pits the servant against the Roman emperor. In so doing he actually follows the lead of the introduction to the fourth Isaianic hymn:

> Behold, my servant shall prosper, he shall be exalted and lifted up, and shall be very high. As many were astonished at him—his appearance was so marred, beyond human semblance, and his form beyond that of the sons of men—so shall he startle many nations; kings shall shut their mouths because of him; for that which has not been told them they shall see, and that which they have not heard they shall understand. (Is 52:13-15)

For how indeed can the Colossians, subjects of the Roman emperor and citizens of Colossae, a mini-Rome, fathom God's representative in terms other than those of the glorious emperor? In turn, this view would have made it impossible for them to accept the portrayal, in those same terms, of someone who was penalized with Roman crucifixion, ultimately through the authority granted by the emperor himself. And yet, this is precisely what Paul is intending to make them hear and submit to. The corollary is that, by accepting Paul's Jesus Christ, the Colossians are opting against Caesar's absolute lordship over them; their citizenry is in the heavenly commonwealth, the residence of the Lord Jesus (Phil 3:20), and their civic behavior is bound by his gospel (1:27). That is why, just as he did in Philippians, after speaking of what Christ did in Isaianic terms (Col 1:15-20; compare with Phil 2:6-11) Paul reminds the Colossians that they are to proceed with their new civic duties (Col 1:21-23; compare with Phil 2:12-13).

---

[26] See *C-Phil* 127-32.

The "divine" terminology of Colossians 1:15-20 is to be understood along the lines of imperial terminology. Julius Caesar was "deified" by decision of the Roman senate as was the first emperor Octavian Caesar Augustus. Subsequent emperors were deified by senatorial decree after their deaths. That the monarch is "divine" is not strange to antiquity. Such a reality is reflected in scripture itself: "I address my verses to the king… Your throne, O God,[27] endures for ever and ever" (Ps 45:1, 6); "For to us a child is born, to us a son is given; and the government will be upon his shoulder, and his name will be called "Wonderful Counselor, Mighty God, Everlasting Father, Prince of Peace." (Is 9:6) However, the monarch's divine status is the result of the Lord's decree issued on the day of enthronement: "I will tell of the decree of the Lord: He said to me, 'You are my son, today I have begotten you.'" (Ps 2:7). What happened in Julius Caesar's times is that the Roman Senate and people (*Senatus populusque Romanus*), that is, the Roman Republic, fell into submission to a human being who masterminded his own deification. And it is ultimately by the authority of such an autocrat, with the consent of the leadership of Jerusalem, the scriptural God's city, that the scriptural God's anointed was condemned to a shameful death. Paul's teaching underscored that this condemnation was proven unjust by God who raised his messenger into his due position of glory and authority (Phil 2:6-11). Here, in Colossians, Paul does the same by depicting Jesus Christ as the true "emperor" to whom the Colossians are to submit.

Unlike the Roman emperor whose authority covers the Roman "habitation" (*oikoumenē*), Jesus Christ's domain extends over the realm of God, whose creation encompasses the heavens and the

---

[27] RSV has "Your divine throne." My translation, however, renders more accurately the original Hebrew.

earth (Gen 1:1). This premise explains Paul's use of a corresponding terminology. Jesus is the "first born" of the entire creation extending over the heavens and the earth (Col 1:15b-17). "First born" (*prōtotokos*) is an honorific title meaning the first in line, similar to the way in the United States the President is referred to as the "first American." Still, the difference is more qualitative than extensive. The scriptural God is unseen since he has no statue depicting him. Consequently, he cannot, logically speaking, reveal "himself." What is revealed to us is his teaching that is communicated to us through his emissary's mouth (Is 6:1-7; 8:16; Jer 1:1-10; Ezek 2:9-3:4). In other words, the scriptural God's reality is reflected in his only representation (*eikōn*) which is the person, or rather the teaching, of his emissary. This is precisely what the deacon declares during the liturgical entrance: it is the Gospel Book that is Christ for the gathered community. Similarly, God "appears" to us through his emissary's words of teaching.[28] Just as God is unseen, so is the lordship of Christ; his lordship is communicated to us through the proclamation of the Pauline gospel embedded in his letters. By trusting Paul's words, the Colossians "see" the glorified Christ. In turn, they cannot "show" to others the Christ whom God glorified; they can only witness to him through their words and, eventually, through their lives. That is why Paul is using a plethora of words to impress on his hearers the universal lordship of Christ not only over whatever they can see (*ta orata*; the matters visible to us) and thus fathom, but also over what lies beyond their horizon (*ta aorata*; the matters invisible to us) (Col 1:16). Finally, to stress his point in an incontrovertible way, he uses (*ta*) *panta* (all things) no less than four times in vv.16-17. All things in the

---

[28] Jer 1:4-10; Ezek 2:1-2; 3:1-4.

entire world are held together by Christ in the same way as all matters in the Roman Empire are held together by the emperor.

Every emperor is first and foremost a Roman patrician, the head of his household. The imperial office is handed down to members of the imperial "household." It is actually through this medium that Julius Caesar handed down the imperial office to Octavian, his niece's son, a member of his "household." The entire patrician system, the heart and soul of the Roman empire, was built around "households." The Roman Senate, whose members were patricians, ruled *urbi et orbi*, the world as well as the city of Rome. Actually it ruled the world through ruling the city of Rome;[29] that is why that empire, as any other empire, *expanded* centrifugally. It is the city of Rome that gave its name to its extensive empire, and not vice-versa. The Roman emperors understood that if their personal households and the households of their supporters in Rome were not in unison, their own hold on the empire would soon end. Put otherwise, the imperial authority over the vast extent of the empire was bound to the emperor's authority over his own household.

Paul, the Roman citizen, perfectly understood this reality, and he made sure that his churches were household churches.[30] His Christ would not be an imperial "universal" Lord (Col 1:15-17) unless and inasmuch as he was first and foremost lord over each and every Pauline household church (vv.18-19). But, beyond the reality of the imperial system, Paul the Pharisee (Phil 3:5) was bred on scripture, and there he learned that, unless God indeed ruled over Israel, he could not be the God of the nations (Rom 9:6-7; 11:1). In critiquing the behavior of the Jew who

---

[29] In the same way, nowadays, world politics as well as United States politics are played out in Washington, D.C.
[30] Rom 16:3-5; 1 Cor 16:19; Col 4:15; Philem 2.

contravenes God's law he quotes Isaiah 52:5: "For, as it is written, 'The name of God is blasphemed among the Gentiles because of you.'" (Rom 2:24) Similarly, Paul is putting pressure on the Colossians who have become through baptism "members of the household (*oikeioi*) of God" (Gal 6:10; Eph 2:19), "which is the church" (1 Tim 3:15; see also vv.3-4), to behave correctly. And the Petrine correspondence, which canonizes Paul's writings as scripture (2 Pet 3:15-16), corroborates their teaching regarding the insiders' being first in line for judgment: "For the time has come for judgment to begin with the house(hold) (*oikou*) of God; and if it begins with us, what will be the end of those who do not obey the gospel of God?" (1 Pet 4:17) This explains Paul's consistent non-pampering intransigence toward the Gentile believers.

After having established the imperial status of Christ (Col 1:15-17), Paul introduces him as the head of the church, using the metaphor of the body which he detailed in 1 Corinthians 12. The entire membership of a Roman household functioned as a body, in unison and harmony, under the one leadership and unquestionable authority (*arkhē*)[31] of the "head," the *paterfamilias*. In scripture, Jesus Christ was "designated, assigned" (*horisthentos*) to that first position (*prōtotokos*; Col 1:18; see also v.15) through God's having "raised him from the dead" (Rom 1:4).[32] Then Paul underscores the fact that Christ's primacy in the empire is intimately linked to his primacy in the household churches: "... *so that* (*hina*) in everything he might be pre-eminent (*prōtevōn*)[33]." (Col 1:18)

---

[31] *arkhē* is weakly translated as "beginning" by RSV.
[32] See also Rev 1:5 for the parallelism between "first born among the dead" and being in the position of unquestionable leadership (*arkhōn*).
[33] From the same root as *prōtotokos*.

Colossians 1:19 (For in him all the fullness was pleased to dwell) together with 2:9 (For in him the whole fullness of deity dwells bodily), I believe, has been misunderstood. This was due to the influence of Platonism and Gnosticism in theological discourse that started with Justin the Philosopher and developed further in the school of Alexandria under the influence of Philo's thought. Instead of keeping the scriptural texts on their original level, which is that of the narrative discourse of the Iliad and the Odyssey, those texts were read as though they had been written *à la* Platonic dialogues. Put otherwise, although scripture deals with God's will and action, it was made into a treatise concerning his "being." Once this was done, scriptural debates then suffered from a constant and consistent *eisegesis* (reading meaning into the text instead of finding the meaning within the text itself). Since most commentators appealed to Gnostic discourse, the assumption was that Colossians 1:19 and 2:9 talked about the being of God and his Christ. But is that indeed so?

In order for us to remain within the scriptural "mood" and thus "mind," we are to submit to the scriptural phraseology of "good pleasure," "fullness," "dwelling," "deity," and "body." The reference "was pleased" is sandwiched between church and the raising of Christ from the dead, on the one hand, and reconciliation and Christ's crucifixion, on the other hand. Taking into consideration both the Pauline corpus and the rest of the New Testament writings, this phraseology reflects, in the divine will, the plan (*oikonomia*) for our ultimate salvation through God's action in Christ. God's "good pleasure" for the Colossians is actually implemented in his "will" to grant them safety from being downtrodden by human imperial hybris through Paul's apostolate to the household church at Colossae run by Epaphras the deacon. Actually, a few verses later, Paul will refer to his apostolate in terms of both "diaconate" and "(household) economy":

> Now I rejoice in my sufferings for your sake, and in my flesh I complete what is lacking in Christ's afflictions for the sake of *his body, that is, the church*, of which I became a minister (*diakonos*; deacon) according to the divine economy (*oikonomian*)[34] which was given to me for you, to fulfill (*plērōsai*) the word of God fully known. (Col 1:24-25)

The parallelism of this phraseology with that of vv.18-19 is unmistakable, and so is the conclusion. Fullness (fulfillment) has to do with God's plan that the Colossians, as well as all the other "saints" in the Roman empire, "fulfill" God's will for them by loving their fellow human beings. Just as God reconciled them to himself through his love for them (Rom 5:1-11), so are they to be reconciled and live in God's—not the Roman—peace with an all-inclusive "all" that encompasses not only the horizon of the Roman empire, but the entirety of God's creation, "the heavens and the earth" (Col 1:20; see also v.16). That is to say, scripturally speaking, all the fullness of God's will is realized when that will abides (dwells) in a household (*katoikēsai*) (Col 1:19; 2:9), with Christ *as head of the church,* (which is) *his* body, and includes the church's membership. Only then the word of God, the gospel preached by Paul (1:5), will be fulfilled (v.25). The addition of "bodily" (*sōmatikōs*) in 2:9 is meant to be understood as "among the entire church membership" and not as an "ontological" reference to the "person" of Christ. This understanding is corroborated in the conclusion (1:21-23) where reference is made to the beginning of the passage: "He is the image of the invisible God, the first-born of all creation (*pasēs ktiseōs*; every creature)" (v.15); "the gospel... which has been

---

[34] From the same root *oik—* as *katoikēsai* (dwell; v.19).

preached to every creature (*pasē ktisei*; all creation) under heaven" (v.23). It is the ultimate result of that reconciliation that counts, which result is the change of the Colossians' *behavior* from "estranged and hostile in mind, *doing evil deeds*" (v.21) into beings that are "holy and blameless and irreproachable" (v.22). This behavior is controlled by the reconciliation that takes place "in the body," that is to say, in the household church where the gospel is heard at every table fellowship, reminding the Colossians of God's will and inviting them to abide by it. And the Colossians had better hearken to that teaching since they shall appear, as in a court room (*parastēsai*; v.22), before God; and it is only he who will deem them *indeed* "holy and blameless and irreproachable." That is why they are to keep trusting in the gospel teaching, in spite of its difficulty. Hearkening to that teaching, heard at every common meal, will preserve them "stable and steadfast, not shifting from the final hope" (v.23) that lies ahead (v.5). Indeed, it is the voice of Paul the minister (*diakonos*; deacon, table servant) that they are hearing, and the message is none other than the message he has been "preaching throughout the entire creation (*en pasei ktēsei*: to every creature) under the heaven" (v.23).

A question that remains is why did Paul write, "he has now reconciled (you have now been reconciled) in the body of his flesh[35] by his death" in v.22? This statement parallels the one just made in v.20 "and through him to reconcile to himself all things, whether on earth or in heaven, making peace by the blood of his cross." The phrase "by the blood of his cross" is as strange as "in the body of his flesh," and they are used in conjunction with reconciliation. Earlier, in discussing v.14 and the passage vv.15-

---

[35] RSV has "in his body of flesh," reflecting the theological teaching on the incarnation, which is not at all within the purview of Colossians 1:15-23.

20, I pointed out to the Isaianic passages relating to the Servant of the Lord as being the background for Paul's teaching. This is corroborated in Ephesians 2:14-20 and two other Pauline passages (Rom 5:1-11; 2 Cor 5:18-20) where similar terminology (peace, enmity, death, blood, remission of sins) is used with the mention of reconciliation. Furthermore, Romans 5:9 refers to "justification through blood," which is the main point of Isaiah 53:10-12, concerning the Servant of the Lord. Justification is the legal verdict pronouncing someone righteous in a court of the law, which is precisely what Paul is speaking of as being the outcome of God's reconciliation through the sacrifice of Christ (Col 1:21-22).

The aspect of an atoning and justifying sacrifice is paramount on Paul's mind in Colossians; this is clear from 1:14 (which mentions redemption, forgiveness of sins) and v.20 (with the mention of blood). Yet these two elements (redemption and blood) are omitted in Philippians, his parallel letter (Phil 2:6-11). This difference is all the more striking when one considers that the "cross," which is at the heart of the Philippians passage, is also on his mind in Colossians. Indeed, in both instances, the "cross" is intentionally underscored since its mention is not necessary, as is clear from the awkward phrases "obedient until death namely, death on the cross" (Phil 2:8) and "by the blood of his cross" (Col 1:20). The solution to understanding the awkward "in the body of his flesh by (the) death" (1:22) is to read it in the light of "by the blood of his cross" (v.20), given that both qualify the divine reconciliation. This is validated in Ephesians 2:14-16, a text that conflates the parallel texts of Colossians 1:20 and 22 into one statement:

> ... and through him to *reconcile* to himself all things, whether on earth or in heaven, *making peace* by the blood of *his cross*. And

> you, who once were estranged and *hostile* in mind, doing evil deeds, he has now reconciled *in the body* of *his flesh* by (his) death... (Col 1:20-22)

> For he is our *peace*, who has made us both one, and has broken down the dividing wall of *hostility* by abolishing *in his flesh* the law of commandments and ordinances, that he might create in himself one new man in place of the two, so *making peace*, and might *reconcile* us both to God *in one body* through *the cross*, thereby bringing the *hostility* to an end. (Eph 2:14-16)

The parallelism between these two passages is even more striking when one reads Ephesians 2:19-22 which is reminiscent of Colossians 1:19 (For in him all the fullness of God was pleased to dwell [*katoikēsai*]) in that it is filled with terms from both the root *oik*— that connotes "house, dwelling" and the root *oikodom*— that connotes the idea of "building":

> So then you are no longer strangers and sojourners (*paroikoi*), but you are fellow citizens with the saints and members of the household (*oikeioi*) of God, built (*epoikodomēthentes*) upon the foundation of the apostles and prophets, Christ Jesus himself being the cornerstone, in whom the whole structure (*oikodomē*) is joined together and grows into a holy temple in the Lord; in whom you also are built into it (*synoikodomeisthe*) for a dwelling place (*katoikētērion*) of God in the Spirit. (Eph 2:19-22)

The conclusion is inevitable. The "body" is the community of the believers and, in Colossians 1:22, it cannot be referring to the physical body of Jesus. Rather, it is "flesh" that has this function. When one takes "flesh" together" with "blood" (v.20), then the pair "flesh and blood" connotes a mere human being (Mt 16:17; 1 Cor 15:50; Gal 1:16; Eph 6:12). Its use in Colossians 1:20-22 makes sense since the entire passage pits the "mere mortal" (flesh and blood) Jesus Christ against the "divine" emperor by showing that God chose the first over the second. When taken in parallel with "by the blood of his cross" (v.20), the phrase "in the body of his flesh by (the) death" (v.22), simply means that in Jesus' death as a mere human being, God reconciled to himself "the body of the church" (see v.18). This reading, as we shall momentarily see, fits perfectly the entire context since, a few verses later, Paul will speak of the sufferings he endures in his own "flesh" in conjunction with Christ's body, the church (v.24).

Vv. 24-29 ²⁴ Νῦν χαίρω ἐν τοῖς παθήμασιν ὑπὲρ ὑμῶν καὶ ἀνταναπληρῶ τὰ ὑστερήματα τῶν θλίψεων τοῦ Χριστοῦ ἐν τῇ σαρκί μου ὑπὲρ τοῦ σώματος αὐτοῦ, ὅ ἐστιν ἡ ἐκκλησία, ²⁵ἧς ἐγενόμην ἐγὼ διάκονος κατὰ τὴν οἰκονομίαν τοῦ θεοῦ τὴν δοθεῖσάν μοι εἰς ὑμᾶς πληρῶσαι τὸν λόγον τοῦ θεοῦ, ²⁶ τὸ μυστήριον τὸ ἀποκεκρυμμένον ἀπὸ τῶν αἰώνων καὶ ἀπὸ τῶν γενεῶν- νῦν δὲ ἐφανερώθη τοῖς ἁγίοις αὐτοῦ, ²⁷ οἷς ἠθέλησεν ὁ θεὸς γνωρίσαι τί τὸ πλοῦτος τῆς δόξης τοῦ μυστηρίου τούτου ἐν τοῖς ἔθνεσιν, ὅ ἐστιν Χριστὸς ἐν ὑμῖν, ἡ ἐλπὶς τῆς δόξης· ²⁸ ὃν ἡμεῖς καταγγέλλομεν νουθετοῦντες πάντα ἄνθρωπον καὶ διδάσκοντες πάντα ἄνθρωπον ἐν πάσῃ σοφίᾳ, ἵνα παραστήσωμεν πάντα ἄνθρωπον τέλειον ἐν Χριστῷ· ²⁹ εἰς ὃ καὶ κοπιῶ ἀγωνιζόμενος κατὰ τὴν ἐνέργειαν αὐτοῦ τὴν ἐνεργουμένην ἐν ἐμοὶ ἐν δυνάμει.

> ²⁴*Now I rejoice in my sufferings for your sake, and in my flesh I complete what is lacking in Christ's afflictions for the sake of his body, that is, the church,* ²⁵*of which I became a minister according to the divine office which was given to me for you, to make the word of God fully known,* ²⁶*the mystery hidden for ages and generations but now made manifest to his saints.* ²⁷*To them God chose to make known how great among the Gentiles are the riches of the glory of this mystery, which is Christ in you, the hope of glory.* ²⁸*Him we proclaim, warning every man and teaching every man in all wisdom, that we may present every man mature in Christ.* ²⁹*For this I toil, striving with all the energy which he mightily inspires within me.*

Since the reconciliation with God through the sacrifice of Christ, on the one hand, and Christ's exaltation as "head" of the created realm, on the other hand, are not visible realities, they are ultimately communicated aurally. Put otherwise, for the Colossians, those realities are made of the actual "words" Paul used to communicate them. As he writes in 1 Corinthians, the meaning as well as reality of the "cross of Christ" (Col 1:20) lies in the "word" that communicates it (1 Cor 1:18), since it is only a "word," and not a piece of wood, that can be voided (of its meaning) (v.17). Consequently, just as in Philippians, the obedience of Christ, the "slave," to God (2:7-8), is reflected in the submission of Paul, the "slave" of Christ (1:1), to that same God, here also the sacrificial death of Christ (Col 1:20, 22) is reflected in Paul's sufferings for the sake of the Colossians (v.24). And these sufferings are directly related to his apostolic activity as is clear from the context: "for the sake of his body, the church (of the Colossians),[36] of which I became a minister (*diakonos*) according to the divine office which was given to me for you, to fulfill (my mission regarding) the word of God." (vv.24-25) That is why, as he does in Philippians (1:18), he rejoices in those sufferings even though he is being spent as a sacrificial offering (2:17). Still, while Christ's sacrifice is already fulfilled since he died, Paul's sacrifice is not yet complete. This explains his "in my flesh (that is to say, as regards to me) I am (still) fulfilling what is lacking in (when compared to) Christ's (fulfilled) afflictions" (Col 1:24); put otherwise, "I am still yearning to follow Christ's example *fully*." This, in no way, is to be understood that Christ's afflictions are lacking, and Paul is fulfilling what was lacking in them. This would blatantly contradict the entire thrust of vv.13-23. What Paul is fulfilling (*antanaplērō*) in v.24 corresponds to

---

[36] That he is thinking of the church community in Colossae is borne out by the similar *hyper* (for the sake of) preceding both "you" and "his body" (v.24).

his fulfilling (*plērōsai*) the word of God among the Colossians (v.25), thus bringing it to full fruition among them (v.6) by having them do every good work (v.10) (of love; v.8) required of them by the gospel (vv.4-5).

In v.26 Paul refers to the gospel, the word of God, as "the mystery hidden for ages and generations but now made manifest to his saints." Very often the term "mystery" has been misconstrued to mean something that remains mysterious and only those who are somehow illumined can comprehend it. In turn, this illumination is viewed as a "spiritual" event to which one accedes under the guidance of a "spiritual" mentor. Such would be a *disciplina arcana* that is revealed only to the chosen few, similar to the priestly *torah* (hidden teaching) which was criticized by God through his *debarim* (open words) that filled his prophets' mouths.[37] Paul comments on this matter at the end of Romans:

> Now to him who is able to strengthen you according to my gospel and the preaching of Jesus Christ, according to the revelation of the mystery which was kept secret for long ages but is now made manifest (*phanerōthentos*) and *through the prophetic writings* is made known (*gnōristhentos*) to all the nations (*eis panta ta ethnē*), according to the command of the eternal God, to bring about the obedience of faith—to the only wise God be glory for evermore through Jesus Christ! Amen. (16:25-26)

The parallelism with Colossians 1:26-27 is evident in the similar terminology:

> ... the mystery hidden for ages and generations but now made manifest (*ephanerōthē*) to his saints, to whom God chose to make known (*gnōrisai*) how great among the Gentiles (*en tois ethnesin*)

---

[37] Jer 1:4-10; Ezek 2:1-2; 3:1-4.

are the riches of the glory of this mystery, which is Christ in you, the hope of glory.

Thus, the mystery Paul is speaking of is not an ontological mystery, but rather a mystery hidden to someone who has not yet been privy to it. In this particular case, the teaching communicated by the prophets is originally a mystery known only to God who then communicated it to his prophets: "Surely the Lord God does nothing, without revealing his (secret) counsel (*sod*) to his servants the prophets. The lion has roared; who will not fear? The Lord God has spoken; who can but prophesy? Proclaim to the strongholds in Assyria, and to the strongholds in the land of Egypt, and say…" (Am 3:7-9a) In turn, when this message is consigned in "the prophetic writings" (Rom 16:26), it ceases to be a mystery to the Jews who "are entrusted with the oracles of God" (3:2). Still the same message remains a mystery to the Gentiles until it is communicated to them by Paul, who is "called to be an apostle, set apart for the gospel of God which he promised beforehand through his prophets in the holy scriptures" (1:1-2). This explication is confirmed in Romans 16:26-27 and in Colossians 1:26-27, with both passages revealing that the mystery specifically concerns "the nations."

Moreover, Christ, God's messiah, who is "among you, Colossians" as he is "among the nations" (Col 1:27; see also v.6) is from the same fabric as his Father and thus the reflection of his Father (v.15). God is "visible" not through a statue representing him, but in the words of scripture; that is why his presence is manifest through hearing and not through seeing. The same applies to his Christ who is "among the nations and the Colossians" to the extent to which Paul's gospel preaching reached their ears (v.5). The close connection in this case between Christ and the gospel is corroborated in that both are linked to the hope of the glory that lies hidden in the heavens (vv.5 and 27). This is further confirmed in that the Christ is said to be proclaimed (*katangellomen*) by Paul (v.28) in the same manner as the mystery and the gospel are: "When I came to you, brethren, I did not come proclaiming (*katangellōn*) to you the mystery[38] of God in lofty words or wisdom" (1 Cor 2:1); "In the same way, the Lord commanded that those who proclaim (*katangellousin*) the gospel should get their living by the gospel." (9:14) Moreover, this proclamation includes not only teaching (*didaskontes*), but also admonishing support (*nouthetountes*) to every human being so that every man may stand perfect on the day of judgment (Col 1:28). Paul is clearly continuing the work done by God through Christ for, just as "he [God] has now reconciled [you] *in the body of his [Christ's] flesh* by his death, in order to present (*parastēsai*) you holy and blameless and irreproachable before him" (v.22), so also "Him [Christ] we proclaim, warning every man and teaching every man in all wisdom, that we may present (*parastēsōmen*) every man perfect *in Christ*" (v.28). The parallelism between these two statements is further enhanced by the correspondence between "in the body of his flesh" in the first instance and, in the second instance, "in Christ," the head of the body (v.18) which is the church (vv.18, 24). In other words, the believer is guaranteed to continue on the right path to the extent he keeps the word of God imparted to him during the house church gatherings. This is ultimately how Paul fulfills what is missing in his flesh as apostle, not so much by devising new ways, but by continuing his apostolic mission:

---

[38] Some manuscripts have "testimony" which amounts to the same thing. In 1 Cor 1:6 Paul refers to the gospel he is preaching as "the mystery of Christ."

"For this I toil (*kopiō*),[39] striving (in the race; *agōnizomenos*) with all his [God's] energy (*energeian*) which is poured (energized; working; *energoumenēn*) in me with power (*en dynamei*)." (v.29) Paul is doing God's work and thus is his co-worker (*synergos*; 1 Cor 3:9).[40] Paul's work will not end until he dies just as God's work in Christ was fulfilled with the latter's death. Until then Paul will continue striving to fulfill what is missing in his flesh, that is to say, he will continue in his personal efforts *as apostle* for the sake of the gospel (Col 1:24) for the remainder of his life.

---

[39] Which is the verb Paul uses to speak of his apostolic activity of preaching the gospel (1 Cor 4:12; 15:10; Gal 4:11; Eph 4:28; Phil 2:16; Col 1:29; 1 Tim 4:10).

[40] *energeian, energoumenēn* and *synergos* are from the same root as the noun *ergon* (work).

Chapter 2

Vv. 1-5 ¹ Θέλω γὰρ ὑμᾶς εἰδέναι ἡλίκον ἀγῶνα ἔχω ὑπὲρ ὑμῶν καὶ τῶν ἐν Λαοδικείᾳ καὶ ὅσοι οὐχ ἑόρακαν τὸ πρόσωπόν μου ἐν σαρκί, ² ἵνα παρακληθῶσιν αἱ καρδίαι αὐτῶν συμβιβασθέντες ἐν ἀγάπῃ καὶ εἰς πᾶν πλοῦτος τῆς πληροφορίας τῆς συνέσεως, εἰς ἐπίγνωσιν τοῦ μυστηρίου τοῦ θεοῦ, Χριστοῦ, ³ ἐν ᾧ εἰσιν πάντες οἱ θησαυροὶ τῆς σοφίας καὶ γνώσεως ἀπόκρυφοι. ⁴ Τοῦτο λέγω, ἵνα μηδεὶς ὑμᾶς παραλογίζηται ἐν πιθανολογίᾳ. ⁵ εἰ γὰρ καὶ τῇ σαρκὶ ἄπειμι, ἀλλὰ τῷ πνεύματι σὺν ὑμῖν εἰμι, χαίρων καὶ βλέπων ὑμῶν τὴν τάξιν καὶ τὸ στερέωμα τῆς εἰς Χριστὸν πίστεως ὑμῶν.

> *¹For I want you to know how greatly I strive for you, and for those at Laodicea, and for all who have not seen my face, ² that their hearts may be encouraged as they are knit together in love, to have all the riches of assured understanding and the knowledge of God's mystery, of Christ, ³in whom are hid all the treasures of wisdom and knowledge. ⁴I say this in order that no one may delude you with beguiling speech. ⁵For though I am absent in body, yet I am with you in spirit, rejoicing to see your good order and the firmness of your faith in Christ.*

Indeed, the race he is running is not only for the Colossians' sake. It is also for those who do not know him but have heard the message from one of his helpers or even through one of his letters (2:1). But why specifically mention the Laodiceans? As I shall show in my discussion of 4:13-16, where the nouns Laodicea and Laodiceans occur no less than four times in four verses, the entire matter revolves around the meaning of Laodicea in Greek: judgment of the people. By bringing into the picture Laodicea as a specific example of a city reached by Paul's gospel, he is reminding the citizens of Colossae, a mini-Rome, and through them the entire empire, that in spite of the fact that it looks as though the Roman emperor rules over the world, that emperor and all his subjects are headed toward the day of judgment by the God and Father of Jesus Christ. Furthermore, as Paul already indicated at the beginning of the letter (1:9-10), even the philosophical wisdom of Greece, which was paramount in the Roman empire, will be of no avail. True wisdom and knowledge are to be found in the scriptural Law that Paul is preaching to the Gentiles (2:2b-3; see also Rom 2:18-20) and that boils down to the love for the neighbor, which ensures unity (*symbibasthentes*) between the citizens of the empire and thus of the empire itself (Col 2:2a). The persuasive speech (*pithanologia*) of Greek rhetorics is actually misleading; Paul states that it misses the mark by speaking *besides* the point (*paralogizētai*) (v.4), since its intent is persuasion for its own sake without consideration of the truth of the matter. By using two terms (*pithanologia* and *paralogizētai*) built around the root *logos* (word) Paul is inviting his hearers to abide at all costs in the gospel "word" in spite of its apparent weakness: "And I was with you in weakness and in much fear and trembling; and my speech and my message were not in plausible words of wisdom, but in demonstration of the Spirit and of power, that your faith might not rest in the wisdom of men but in the power of God." (1 Cor 2:3-5) The Colossians are to remain in this same spirit, even in his absence, and, consequently, such firmness (*stereōma*) [in steadfastness] will ensure the good order (*taxin*) within every household committed to Christ (Col 2:5).

Vv. 6-15 ⁶ Ὡς οὖν παρελάβετε τὸν Χριστὸν Ἰησοῦν τὸν κύριον, ἐν αὐτῷ περιπατεῖτε, ⁷ ἐρριζωμένοι καὶ ἐποικοδομούμενοι ἐν αὐτῷ καὶ βεβαιούμενοι τῇ πίστει καθὼς ἐδιδάχθητε, περισσεύοντες ἐν εὐχαριστίᾳ. ⁸ Βλέπετε μή τις ὑμᾶς ἔσται ὁ συλαγωγῶν διὰ τῆς φιλοσοφίας καὶ κενῆς ἀπάτης κατὰ τὴν παράδοσιν τῶν ἀνθρώπων, κατὰ τὰ στοιχεῖα τοῦ κόσμου καὶ οὐ κατὰ Χριστόν· ⁹ ὅτι ἐν αὐτῷ κατοικεῖ πᾶν τὸ πλήρωμα τῆς θεότητος σωματικῶς, ¹⁰ καὶ ἐστὲ ἐν αὐτῷ πεπληρωμένοι, ὅς ἐστιν ἡ κεφαλὴ πάσης ἀρχῆς καὶ

Chapter 2

ἐξουσίας. ¹¹ Ἐν ᾧ καὶ περιετμήθητε περιτομῇ ἀχειροποιήτῳ ἐν τῇ ἀπεκδύσει τοῦ σώματος τῆς σαρκός, ἐν τῇ περιτομῇ τοῦ Χριστοῦ, ¹² συνταφέντες αὐτῷ ἐν τῷ βαπτισμῷ, ἐν ᾧ καὶ συνηγέρθητε διὰ τῆς πίστεως τῆς ἐνεργείας τοῦ θεοῦ τοῦ ἐγείραντος αὐτὸν ἐκ νεκρῶν· ¹³ καὶ ὑμᾶς νεκροὺς ὄντας [ἐν] τοῖς παραπτώμασιν καὶ τῇ ἀκροβυστίᾳ τῆς σαρκὸς ὑμῶν, συνεζωοποίησεν ὑμᾶς σὺν αὐτῷ, χαρισάμενος ἡμῖν πάντα τὰ παραπτώματα. ¹⁴ ἐξαλείψας τὸ καθ' ἡμῶν χειρόγραφον τοῖς δόγμασιν ὃ ἦν ὑπεναντίον ἡμῖν, καὶ αὐτὸ ἦρκεν ἐκ τοῦ μέσου προσηλώσας αὐτὸ τῷ σταυρῷ· ¹⁵ ἀπεκδυσάμενος τὰς ἀρχὰς καὶ τὰς ἐξουσίας ἐδειγμάτισεν ἐν παρρησίᾳ, θριαμβεύσας αὐτοὺς ἐν αὐτῷ.

> ⁶As therefore you received Christ Jesus the Lord, so live in him, ⁷rooted and built up in him and established in the faith, just as you were taught, abounding in thanksgiving. ⁸See to it that no one makes a prey of you by philosophy and empty deceit, according to human tradition, according to the elemental spirits of the universe, and not according to Christ. ⁹For in him the whole fulness of deity dwells bodily, ¹⁰and you have come to fulness of life in him, who is the head of all rule and authority. ¹¹In him also you were circumcised with a circumcision made without hands, by putting off the body of flesh in the circumcision of Christ; ¹²and you were buried with him in baptism, in which you were also raised with him through faith in the working of God, who raised him from the dead. ¹³And you, who were dead in trespasses and the uncircumcision of your flesh, God made alive together with him, having forgiven us all our trespasses, ¹⁴having canceled the bond which stood against us with its legal demands; this he set aside, nailing it to the cross. ¹⁵He disarmed the principalities and powers and made a public example of them, triumphing over them in him.

Good order will be maintained so long as the Colossians "walk" according to the will of Christ Jesus who has become, through the gospel message they received, their new household lord (2:6). To elucidate his teaching Paul uses his two classic metaphors of plant and building to speak of that new household, the house church (1 Cor 3:1-17). Indeed, the Colossians are to be "rooted and built up (upon)" in Christ, that is to say, firmly established in the trust they have put in Paul's teaching (Col 2:7). However, their own efforts are not to be viewed as though they originated with them since "God is at work in you, both to will and to work for his good pleasure" (Phil 2:13). That is why their attitude has to be one of thanksgiving to God himself (Col 2:7) after the manner of Paul, who thanks God, not the Colossians, for their response to his preaching (1:3-4). In 2:8-9, Paul revisits what he referred to earlier as "persuasive talk" (*pithanologia*; beguiling speech) in vv.3-5, here naming it outright "philosophy":

> ... in whom [Christ] are hid all the treasures of wisdom (*sophias*) and knowledge. I say this in order that no one may delude you with beguiling speech (*pithanologia*). (2:3-4)

> See to it that no one makes a prey of you (*sylagōgōn*) by philosophy (*philosophias*) and empty deceit, according to human tradition, according to the elemental spirits of the universe (*ta stoikheia tou kosmou*), and not according to Christ. For in him the whole fullness of deity dwells bodily... (2:8-9)

Philosophy is deceiving because its power is not as readily overwhelming as that of the Roman emperor. It purports to be reflective of wisdom, which is supposed to be ultimately the product of a superior intellect and thus, in the public mind, of the gods. The most striking case in point is the goddess Athena, goddess of wisdom and patron of Athens, the city of Socrates, Plato, and Aristotle. The Book of Acts reflects that the gospel message was dismissed by the philosophers of that city (17:18-20). Since the gospel, and the *torah* it carries, is a teaching, it stands to reason that its deadliest enemy is not so much Roman power as it is Greek philosophical thought. The entire scriptural literature of the Writings was conceived around the premise that the *torah* was true wisdom.[1] Even the Book of Daniel in the Writings, which speaks of God's superior power over that of empires, casts its hero as a wise man similar to Joseph in Egypt. The pernicious enmity of philosophy is evidenced through Paul's use of the verb *sylagōgō,* unique in the New Testament, which is a military term that means "to force someone into captivity after having submitted him to the spoil of defeat." To speak of false teaching, dubbed as a tradition of men and not of God, is reminiscent of Galatians (1:6; 2:4; 5:25).[2] Galatians was definitely on the writer's mind since the phrase "the elemental spirits of this world" (*ta stoikheia tou kosmou*; Col 2:8, 20) is found elsewhere only in Galatians 4:3 (and also in v.9 as *stoikheia*), and in both cases as opposed to what God did for the Gentiles through Christ.

In Galatians "the elemental spirits" parallel the pagan idols: "Formerly, when you did not know God, you were in bondage to beings that by nature are no gods; but now that you have come to know God, or rather to be known by God, how can you turn back again to the weak and beggarly elemental spirits, whose slaves you want to be once more?" (4:8-9) Consequently, what Paul is trying to say in Colossians 2:8a-9, as I explained earlier in conjunction with 1:19, is that divine wisdom, which is the supposed fullness of the wisdom of the gods, is not to be found in Greek philosophy, but in the teaching heard in the body of Christ, that is, at table fellowship in the house churches where Paul's gospel is expounded. It is there, and not at Roman or Greek academies, where the Colossians are filled with the teaching and thus the presence of Christ, their *paterfamilias* and

---

[1] See *OTI₃* 121-28.
[2] See my comments on those verses in *Gal* 27-31, 63-66, 304-05.

emperor (2:10). And, in order to differentiate his house churches from the synagogues and from the gatherings of his opponents, Paul adds what he already launched in Galatians (3:26-28), namely, that baptism takes the place of circumcision (Col 2:11-12).

Since the Colossian church is the temple (building) of God (v.7) not made by man's hand (Mk 14:58), its membership is Abraham's seed (Gal 3:29) through baptism (vv.27-28), which is viewed as a circumcision of the heart. Through baptism one becomes a member of the Pauline church "body" that includes Gentiles as well as Jews, rather than a member of the synagogue "body" reserved to those who undergo circumcision in the "flesh." Paul metaphorically speaks of baptism, the "circumcision of (through) Christ" (Col 2:11), as "putting on" Christ (Gal 3:27), that is to say, wearing his household garb; and if one does so, then he "puts off" the garb of the household ("body") defined by circumcision in the flesh (Col 2:11). The other metaphor used concerning baptism (vv. 12-13) corresponds to the one developed in Romans 6. In baptism we are co-buried with Christ and thus have the hope of being raised unto eternal life by the same God who showed his power to do so by raising Christ from the dead (Col 2:12). The Colossians will have access to that life so long they lead a new kind of life void of the sins they perpetrated while they were uncircumcised and from which they were absolved through God's sheer graciousness (Col 2:13). The repeated use in v.13 of "trespasses" (*paraptōmata*) instead of "sins" that was used in 1:14 is intentional. It prepares for 2:14 where we are told that the Colossians have been absolved of the potential punishment prescribed by the Law against such infractions.

Verses 12-13 have often been erroneously taken to mean that the Colossians were co-raised and thus already raised and share eternal life with Christ. Such an interpretation has led to endless discussions about "realized eschatology" or at least "inaugurated eschatology." If such were the case, then the teaching in Colossians 2 would contradict that in Romans 6-8. The reason behind the misreading lies in the value of the "aorist" Greek verbal form. Recent language studies have shown that verbal forms are to be approached modally, from the perspective of the action, rather than temporally, from the perspective of time divided into past, present, and future. Take, for instance, the English, "I shall have eaten" or even simply "having eaten." Is the action of eating already consummated or not? The "have eaten" militates for the former, whereas the "shall" for the latter. The dilemma is solved only when one approaches the matter not temporally, but views the action of eating in conjunction with another action: "After I shall have eaten (having eaten), I shall go to the movies." The eating is before the going, yet it is still in the future. Thus functions the "aorist," which is a transliteration of *aoristos* meaning "without horizon, non-delineated, undefined." It is essentially a modal verbal form expressing the completeness of the action disregarding the time element. Consequently, it expresses the assuredness of the action referred to rather than the time it takes place. And this is precisely what Colossians 2:12-13 is trying to convey: assuredness provided the Colossians maintain their resolve, which will be confirmed in the following verses where Paul asks them to behave in a certain manner. To further illustrate my point, let me quote the striking instance of Romans 8:24-25: "For in this hope *we were saved* (*esōthēmen* [aorist]). Now hope that is seen is not hope. For who hopes for what he sees? But if we hope for what we do not see, we wait for it with patience." The salvation Paul is speaking of in these verses lies ahead, yet it is expressed in the aorist tense, which reflects the assuredness of our salvation *should we wait with patience.* This understanding is corroborated in what Paul wrote a few verses earlier: "For you did not receive the spirit of slavery to fall back into fear, but you have received the spirit of sonship. When we cry 'Abba! Father!' it is the Spirit himself bearing witness with our spirit that we are children of God, and if children, then heirs, heirs of God and fellow heirs with Christ, *provided we suffer with him in order that we may also be glorified with him.*"(vv.15-17)

Once again it seems that Galatians was on the author's mind in the wording of Colossians 2:12-14:

> ... in which [baptism] you were also raised with him through faith in the working of God, who raised him from the dead. And you, who were dead in trespasses and the uncircumcision of your flesh, God made alive together with him, having freely forgiven (*kharisamenos*) us all our trespasses, having canceled the bond (*kheirographon*; certificate of indebtedness) which stood against us with its legal demands; this he set aside (*ērken ek tou mesou*; lifted from the midst), nailing it to the cross.

The outcome of the crucifixion is the blessing promised by the Law to the Jews and the Gentiles that their trespasses will be forgiven, as long as they put their trust in that message of blessing and forgiveness. The combination of the annulment of the curse linked to the failure to abide by the Law's commandments, on the one hand, and the crucifixion, on the other hand, is found elsewhere in the New Testament only in Galatians:

> Christ redeemed us from the curse of the law, having become a curse for us—for it is written, "Cursed be every one who hangs on a tree"— that in Christ Jesus the blessing of Abraham might come

upon the Gentiles, that we might receive the promise of the Spirit through faith. (3:13-14)

The correspondence is even more striking when in Colossians, beginning with "having graciously forgiven" (*kharisamenos*; 2:13), we have a shift from the second person plural, referring to the Gentile Colossians (vv.6-13a), to the first person plural that includes the Jew Paul and his Jewish colleagues (vv.13b-14). In my discussion of Galatians 3:13-14 I have shown that the "us," used twice (v.13), refers to the Jews and, after the mention of the Gentiles in v.14a, the "we" of v.14b is inclusive of both Jews and Gentiles.[3]

The question that remains is, "What does the phrase 'lifted from the midst' (*herken ek tou mesou*) which RSV translates as 'set aside' (Col. 2:14), refer to?" If God cancelled and also lifted the bond that stood *against* us, due to our trespasses, then the "midst" is between God and us. And, since "both Jews and Greeks are under the power of sin" (Rom 3:9) and thus guilty of trespasses, the differentiation between Jew and Gentile is eliminated. Consequently, the "midst" also refers to the separation between Jew and Gentile, which is lifted. My reading is corroborated in the parallel extended passage in Ephesians:

> Therefore remember that at one time you Gentiles in the flesh, called the uncircumcision by what is called the circumcision, which is made in the flesh by hands—remember that you were at that time separated from Christ, alienated from the commonwealth of Israel, and strangers to the covenants of promise, having no hope and without God in the world. But now in Christ Jesus you who once were far off have been brought near in the blood of Christ. For he is our peace, who has made us both

---

[3] See *Gal* 129-37.

one, and has broken down the dividing wall (*to mesotoikhon*)[4] of hostility, by abolishing in his flesh the law of commandments and ordinances, that he might create in himself one new man in place of the two, so making peace, and might reconcile us both to God in one body through the cross, thereby bringing the hostility to an end. And he came and preached peace to you who were far off and peace to those who were near; for through him we both have access in one Spirit to the Father. (2:11-18)

As always, Paul's world of reference is the Roman empire, and not a theoretical ontological world of Jew versus Gentile. That is why, after having established the oneness of the Jew and the Gentile in the same household church, he goes back to underscoring that this new reality is not under the authority of Caesar, but is under that of God's crucified messiah, who is both emperor and *paterfamilias*. Indeed, Christ became the head of all rule (*arkhēs*) and authority (*exousias*) (Col 2:10) since God disarmed all principalities (*arkhas*; ruling powers) and powers (*exousias*; authorities) and triumphed over them publicly in Christ (v.15). "Disarmed" is the translation of the Greek *apekdysamenos* (took off their clothing), which is the same verb used earlier in v.11 to speak of "putting off the body of flesh." The hearer cannot miss this link which confirms Paul's intent to say that Christ has become functionally for the believers the true emperor and *paterfamilias*, that is to say, the head of both the empire and every believing household in it.

Vv. 16-23 ¹⁶ Μὴ οὖν τις ὑμᾶς κρινέτω ἐν βρώσει καὶ ἐν πόσει ἢ ἐν μέρει ἑορτῆς ἢ νεομηνίας ἢ σαββάτων· ¹⁷ ἅ ἐστιν σκιὰ τῶν μελλόντων, τὸ δὲ σῶμα τοῦ Χριστοῦ. ¹⁸ μηδεὶς ὑμᾶς καταβραβευέτω θέλων ἐν ταπεινοφροσύνῃ καὶ θρησκείᾳ τῶν ἀγγέλων, ἃ ἑόρακεν ἐμβατεύων, εἰκῇ φυσιούμενος ὑπὸ

---

[4] The first part *meso—* of the noun *mesotoikhon* is from the same root as *mesou* (midst) in Col 2:14.

τοῦ νοὸς τῆς σαρκὸς αὐτοῦ, ¹⁹ καὶ οὐ κρατῶν τὴν κεφαλήν, ἐξ οὗ πᾶν τὸ σῶμα διὰ τῶν ἁφῶν καὶ συνδέσμων ἐπιχορηγούμενον καὶ συμβιβαζόμενον αὔξει τὴν αὔξησιν τοῦ θεοῦ. ²⁰ Εἰ ἀπεθάνετε σὺν Χριστῷ ἀπὸ τῶν στοιχείων τοῦ κόσμου, τί ὡς ζῶντες ἐν κόσμῳ δογματίζεσθε; ²¹ μὴ ἅψῃ μηδὲ γεύσῃ μηδὲ θίγῃς, ²² ἅ ἐστιν πάντα εἰς φθορὰν τῇ ἀποχρήσει, κατὰ τὰ ἐντάλματα καὶ διδασκαλίας τῶν ἀνθρώπων, ²³ ἅτινά ἐστιν λόγον μὲν ἔχοντα σοφίας ἐν ἐθελοθρησκίᾳ καὶ ταπεινοφροσύνῃ [καὶ] ἀφειδίᾳ σώματος, οὐκ ἐν τιμῇ τινι πρὸς πλησμονὴν τῆς σαρκός.

¹⁶Therefore let no one pass judgment on you in questions of food and drink or with regard to a festival or a new moon or a sabbath. ¹⁷These are only a shadow of what is to come; but the substance belongs to Christ. ¹⁸Let no one disqualify you, insisting on self-abasement and worship of angels, taking his stand on visions, puffed up without reason by his sensuous mind, ¹⁹and not holding fast to the Head, from whom the whole body, nourished and knit together through its joints and ligaments, grows with a growth that is from God. ²⁰If with Christ you died to the elemental spirits of the universe, why do you live as if you still belonged to the world? Why do you submit to regulations, ²¹"Do not handle, Do not taste, Do not touch" ²²(referring to things which all perish as they are used), according to human precepts and doctrines? ²³These have indeed an appearance of wisdom in promoting rigor of devotion and self-abasement and severity to the body, but they are of no value in checking the indulgence of the flesh.

Again, as he does in Galatians (4:8-10), here Paul warns the Colossians, who were freed from all powers and authorities, not to fall prey to any disguised form of enslavement, which would be tantamount to being again under "the elemental spirits of the universe" (Col 2:20). If the God of scripture liberated the Colossians, then they are not to submit to the Jerusalemite leaders whose interest is to Judaize them. The immediate connection with Galatians is evident in that the leading elements which Paul addresses are "eating and drinking" (Col 2:16), which is the heart of the Antioch controversy (Gal 2:11-14). Since Colossians has proven time and again to be patterned after Galatians, which will be fully as well as further confirmed in Colossians 3:11 (where there cannot be Greek and Jew, circumcised and uncircumcised, barbarian, Scythian, slave, free man, but Christ is all, and in all), it would behoove us to read verses 2:16-19 in light of that letter.

In Galatians Paul put under question the authority of the Jerusalemite leaders who, reminiscent of the kings of Jerusalem of old, were trying to control their subjects in the name of the capital city and its temple where the Lord was made to reside. But, according to the witness of scripture, the book of the Law where God's will was inscribed actually was buried under the stones of that temple and thus his commandments were never heeded (2 Kg 22:1-13; 23:21-22). Similar to the kings of old, Paul's contemporary Jerusalem leaders were interested in the number of circumcised in order to secure the levy of more taxes for the building of the temple. Thus they were using others for their own glory: "For even those who receive circumcision do not themselves keep the law, but they desire to have you circumcised that they may glory in your flesh." (Gal 6:13) In the name of the earthly passing Jerusalem, they were enslaving those who were slated to be the children of the Jerusalem above (Gal 4:25-26), of which Isaiah speaks. But, again according to scripture, the earthly temple is supposed to be the blueprint of the heavenly one, not vice versa (Ex 25:40; 26:30; 27:8). The prophets repeatedly reminded their people that, ultimately, God was in no need of a stone building (Is 66:1-2) to gather his children. To the contrary, "For it is written, 'Rejoice, O barren one who does not bear; break forth and shout, you who are not in travail; for the children of the desolate one are many more than the children of her that is married'" (Gal 4:27; Is 54:1).

Thus, scripturally speaking, God's plan sketched in the Mosaic law falters in the story of Israel in Canaan, a story that starts with the allotment of the land to the tribes (Josh 14-19), but sadly ends in the destruction of Jerusalem and the exile (2 Kg 25). The plan's actual realization takes place only in the hope expressed in the Latter Prophets, when the nations will join the repentant Israel in submission to the will of God that will make out of them children of the new heavenly Jerusalem (Isaiah), which Paul speaks of in Galatians 4:26-27 as being the realization of God's promise to Abraham (v.28). So, in that sense, (1) no one is to emit judgment against the Colossians in matters of the Law (Col 2:16), and (2) the Law's requirements are the shadow (reflection) of *the things to come* (*tōn mellontōn*; v.17a). In order to understand what is meant by this phrase one is to recall Ezekiel, who dubs God's metaphorical city "the Lord is there" at the closure of his book (48:35). What is interesting in Ezekiel's handling of the matter, however, is that this city is the only city in the land that is allotted to the tribes as an open pasture (Ezek 48). Such is to be expected since God, who was unhappy with the kings of Judah and Israel, dismissed those two kingdoms with their cities and became himself the shepherd of his people before choosing a new representative, a new David, who would shepherd the people (Ezek 34). If the new city "the Lord is there" replaced Jerusalem that started in 2 Samuel 5, then the pasture land looks back to the beginning of the story in Joshua, the first Book of the Former Prophets, where the tribal lots were filled with cities (Josh 14-20). Those cities ended up as mere shadows among the rubble. Paradoxically, the reality actually lay in the Ezekelian picture of sheep finding life and peace in an open land of pasture, where they graze unharmed under the watchful eye of their shepherd in his city (Ezek 48:30-35) not made by the hand of man (Is 66:1-2).

Such land of pasture is obviously metaphoric. Its actuality encompassed the open extant of the earth where the disciples of Ezekiel, though scattered away from their land, found the "actuality" of life and peace granted to them by God whenever they congregated around God *in the reading of his law* on the sabbath. The congregation was called "synagogue" (Greek *synagōgē*; Hebrew *'edah*; coming together) which is one of the two main appellations of God's assembly. Paul opted to speak of his mainly Gentile congregations with the other term "church" (Greek *ekklēsia*; Hebrew *qahal*; gathering) for two reasons. First of all, the appellation "synagogue" risked that the Pauline churches would slip more readily in Peter's camp (Gal 2:7-8) and, by the same token, under the aegis of James and the Jerusalemite leadership (vv.11-14). Secondly, the term *ekklēsia* was the common name of the Greco-Roman city's body politic and had an appeal to the Gentiles in that it would not sound for them as though they were uprooted; they would, *as Gentiles*— without being forced into circumcision—become members of the scriptural God's household (6:10) and join in "the Israel of God" (v.16; Eph 2:11-13). This reading, I believe, accounts for the mention in Colossians 2:16 of "sabbaths,[5]" which is a unique instance in the Pauline corpus and which seems to prepare for the statement "a shadow of the things to come; but the substance (*sōma*) belongs to Christ" (v.17). So Paul was asking the Colossians not to accept to be forced into going to the synagogues on the sabbaths to hear God's law, but to consider their own house gatherings as the new "substance" (*sōma*; reality) since in those Pauline gatherings Gentiles and Jews shared the same table fellowship in the way Isaiah foresaw would prevail in the "new Jerusalem."

---

[5] The Greek has the plural "sabbaths."

The eschatological community of God's people that includes the nations was introduced thrice as "the body of Christ" (Col 1:18, 24; 2:9). So, in preparation for the recalling of this metaphor in 2:19, Paul uses the "body" in v.17 as being the opposite or, more appropriately, the reality of the shadow, which is a perfect usage of the Greek. Just as is the case with the English "body," the Greek *sōma* reflects the actual physical and thus tangible reality of something. One does not bump into the shadow of a chair, for instance, whereas one bumps into (the actual body of) that same chair. So what Paul is saying in v.17 is that *the things to come*, that is to say, the promise we are awaiting to be realized, is taking shape in the household whose head is Christ and will take final shape at his coming. As Paul states in Philippians: "But our commonwealth is in heaven, and from it *we await* a Savior, the Lord Jesus Christ, who will change our lowly body to be like his glorious body, by the power which enables him even to subject all things to himself." (3:20-21) That Paul is speaking of something that lies ahead of the Colossians is corroborated by his warning that they not be duped by anyone who would want to "disqualify" (*katabrabetō*; rob [someone] of the *winner's prize*) them of the prize (*brabeion*, from the same root as *katabrabetō*) that lies above as well as ahead: "Brethren, I do not consider that I have made it my own; but one thing I do, forgetting what lies behind and straining forward to what lies ahead, I press on toward the goal for the prize (*brabeion*) of the upward call of God in Christ Jesus." (Phil 3:13-14) That is why, later in Colossians, Paul writes: "And let the peace of Christ rule (*brabetō*; functions as the prize sought after) in your hearts, to which indeed you were called *in the one body*. And be thankful." (Col 3:15) The peace to which they are called is the coming Kingdom that lies ahead.

In spite of their apparent humility, those who are trying to deceive the Colossians appeal to a religious behavior originating with angels, to which the deceivers say they were privy through (heavenly) visions. In reality they are puffed up (*physioumenos*) in their human (fleshly) mind (2:18). In other words, even though they attribute their false teaching to divine authority, it is nothing more than "the tradition of men" (2:8). The same terminology of "visions" and "being puffed up" (*physiōseis*; conceit) is found in chapter 12 of 2 Corinthians (visions in v.1 and conceit in v.20) where Paul belittles the importance of visions after having criticized the arrogance of the "false apostles" as being "the ministers (deacons) of Satan," whom he dubs as "angel of light" (11:13-15). However, it is in 1 Corinthians that we find the highest incidence of the root *physio*— (puff up; 4:6; 8:1; 13:4). These instances are telling; the last two instances are made in conjunction with love, which is the central point of behavior required from the Colossians and secured through the watchful eye of the "deacon" (table minister) Epaphras (Col 1:7-8). Moreover, the verb contrary to "puff up" in 1 Cor 8:1 is "upbuild," which in chapter 12 is spoken of in terms of body and occurs frequently in chapter 14 in reference to the church. In 1 Cor 4:6, the root *physio*— occurs in conjunction with the table fellowship community and "(temple) building." Paul uses "(temple) building" and "body" as metaphors for the house church in Colossians. The correspondence between Colossians and 1-2 Corinthians, as well as Galatians, is striking. One cannot but conclude that Colossians 2:16-19 are aimed at Paul's opponents who are trying to dismantle the house churches he is so diligently founding and maintaining.

The true apostle, as Paul depicts him in 2 Corinthians 11 and 12, does not glory falsely in his "divinely inspired visions." Rather he holds firmly to Christ, the head of the body (Col

2:19) in whom the fullness of God was pleased to dwell bodily (1:19; 2:9). This Christ is exclusively communicated through the Pauline teaching (2:6-7). That teaching underscores that Christ does not lie in a Platonic heaven of ideas, but rather in a heaven "ahead" whence he comes to judge whether the members of his household will have abided in the behavior required from them. Indeed, the body of which Paul speaks in v.19 is a not an anatomical metaphor whereby the head is merely the central organ, but a body that grows "out of" (*ex*) its head, being nourished (*epikhorēgoumenon*; provided for, supported by [God])[6] and knit together (*symbibazomenon*; united)[7] "through" (*dia*) the joints and ligaments; moreover the body's growth is willed by God. Such terminology used to describe this body fits that of a Roman patrician who unites as well as rules over his household through his teaching and directives.

In order to bring his point as close to home as possible, Paul recapitulates what he wrote in vv.6-19 in the form of a lengthy rhetorical question followed by a statement, both of which are replete with the terminology extant in those verses:

> If with Christ you died [v.12] to the elemental spirits of the universe (v.8), why do you live [v.13] as if you still belonged to the world? Why do you submit to regulations [v.14],[8] "Do not handle, Do not taste [v.16], Do not touch," referring to things which all perish as they are used, according to human precepts and doctrines [v.8]? These seem indeed to be a word of wisdom[9] in promoting rigor of devotion and self-abasement [v.18] and

---

[6] Compare with 2 Cor 9:10 [twice]; Gal 3:5; Phil 1:19; 1 Pet 4:11; 2 Pet 1:11.
[7] Compare with Col 2:2.
[8] The verb *dogmatizesthe* (make regulations; v.20) is from the same root as *dogmasin* (legal demands; v.14).
[9] Contrast with 1:9, 28; 2:3

severity to the body, but they are of no value in checking the indulgence of the *flesh* [vv.11, 13, 18]. (Col 2:20-23)

Chapter 3

Vv. 1-17 ¹ Εἰ οὖν συνηγέρθητε τῷ Χριστῷ, τὰ ἄνω ζητεῖτε, οὗ ὁ Χριστός ἐστιν ἐν δεξιᾷ τοῦ θεοῦ καθήμενος· ² τὰ ἄνω φρονεῖτε, μὴ τὰ ἐπὶ τῆς γῆς. ³ ἀπεθάνετε γὰρ καὶ ἡ ζωὴ ὑμῶν κέκρυπται σὺν τῷ Χριστῷ ἐν τῷ θεῷ. ⁴ ὅταν ὁ Χριστὸς φανερωθῇ, ἡ ζωὴ ὑμῶν, τότε καὶ ὑμεῖς σὺν αὐτῷ φανερωθήσεσθε ἐν δόξῃ. ⁵ Νεκρώσατε οὖν τὰ μέλη τὰ ἐπὶ τῆς γῆς, πορνείαν ἀκαθαρσίαν πάθος ἐπιθυμίαν κακήν, καὶ τὴν πλεονεξίαν, ἥτις ἐστὶν εἰδωλολατρία, ⁶ δι' ἃ ἔρχεται ἡ ὀργὴ τοῦ θεοῦ [ἐπὶ τοὺς υἱοὺς τῆς ἀπειθείας]. ⁷ ἐν οἷς καὶ ὑμεῖς περιεπατήσατέ ποτε, ὅτε ἐζῆτε ἐν τούτοις· ⁸ νυνὶ δὲ ἀπόθεσθε καὶ ὑμεῖς τὰ πάντα, ὀργήν, θυμόν, κακίαν, βλασφημίαν, αἰσχρολογίαν ἐκ τοῦ στόματος ὑμῶν· ⁹ μὴ ψεύδεσθε εἰς ἀλλήλους, ἀπεκδυσάμενοι τὸν παλαιὸν ἄνθρωπον σὺν ταῖς πράξεσιν αὐτοῦ ¹⁰ καὶ ἐνδυσάμενοι τὸν νέον τὸν ἀνακαινούμενον εἰς ἐπίγνωσιν κατ' εἰκόνα τοῦ κτίσαντος αὐτόν, ¹¹ὅπου οὐκ ἔνι Ἕλλην καὶ Ἰουδαῖος, περιτομὴ καὶ ἀκροβυστία, βάρβαρος, Σκύθης, δοῦλος, ἐλεύθερος, ἀλλὰ [τὰ] πάντα καὶ ἐν πᾶσιν Χριστός. ¹² Ἐνδύσασθε οὖν, ὡς ἐκλεκτοὶ τοῦ θεοῦ ἅγιοι καὶ ἠγαπημένοι, σπλάγχνα οἰκτιρμοῦ χρηστότητα ταπεινοφροσύνην πραΰτητα μακροθυμίαν, ¹³ ἀνεχόμενοι ἀλλήλων καὶ χαριζόμενοι ἑαυτοῖς ἐάν τις πρός τινα ἔχῃ μομφήν· καθὼς καὶ ὁ κύριος ἐχαρίσατο ὑμῖν, οὕτως καὶ ὑμεῖς· ¹⁴ ἐπὶ πᾶσιν δὲ τούτοις τὴν ἀγάπην, ὅ ἐστιν σύνδεσμος τῆς τελειότητος. ¹⁵ καὶ ἡ εἰρήνη τοῦ Χριστοῦ βραβευέτω ἐν ταῖς καρδίαις ὑμῶν, εἰς ἣν καὶ ἐκλήθητε ἐν ἑνὶ σώματι· καὶ εὐχάριστοι γίνεσθε. ¹⁶ Ὁ λόγος τοῦ Χριστοῦ ἐνοικείτω ἐν ὑμῖν πλουσίως, ἐν πάσῃ σοφίᾳ διδάσκοντες καὶ νουθετοῦντες ἑαυτούς, ψαλμοῖς ὕμνοις ᾠδαῖς πνευματικαῖς ἐν [τῇ] χάριτι ᾄδοντες ἐν ταῖς καρδίαις ὑμῶν τῷ θεῷ. ¹⁷ καὶ πᾶν ὅ τι ἐὰν ποιῆτε ἐν λόγῳ ἢ ἐν ἔργῳ, πάντα ἐν ὀνόματι κυρίου Ἰησοῦ, εὐχαριστοῦντες τῷ θεῷ πατρὶ δι' αὐτοῦ.

¹*If then you have been raised with Christ, seek the things that are above, where Christ is, seated at the right hand of God.* ²*Set your minds on things that are above, not on things that are on earth.* ³*For*

you have died, and your life is hid with Christ in God. ⁴When Christ who is our life appears, then you also will appear with him in glory. ⁵Put to death therefore what is earthly in you: fornication, impurity, passion, evil desire, and covetousness, which is idolatry. ⁶On account of these the wrath of God is coming. ⁷In these you once walked, when you lived in them. ⁸But now put them all away: anger, wrath, malice, slander, and foul talk from your mouth. ⁹Do not lie to one another, seeing that you have put off the old nature with its practices ¹⁰and have put on the new nature, which is being renewed in knowledge after the image of its creator. ¹¹Here there cannot be Greek and Jew, circumcised and uncircumcised, barbarian, Scythian, slave, free man, but Christ is all, and in all. ¹²Put on then, as God's chosen ones, holy and beloved, compassion, kindness, lowliness, meekness, and patience, ¹³forbearing one another and, if one has a complaint against another, forgiving each other; as the Lord has forgiven you, so you also must forgive. ¹⁴And above all these put on love, which binds everything together in perfect harmony. ¹⁵And let the peace of Christ rule in your hearts, to which indeed you were called in the one body. And be thankful. ¹⁶Let the word of Christ dwell in you richly, teach and admonish one another in all wisdom, and sing psalms and hymns and spiritual songs with thankfulness in your hearts to God. ¹⁷And whatever you do, in word or deed, do everything in the name of the Lord Jesus, giving thanks to God the Father through him.

Since this recapitulation covered the negative past, Paul moves to the positive aspect of the same teaching, that is, the kind of life the Colossians are to lead. Given that Christ, their new paterfamilias, is now seated as the guest of honor at the right hand of God, the Colossians who, through Christ, have the assurance that they will eventually share fully in that table fellowship, are to lead a life worthy of their "head." He is "above" and they are to seek the matters above. In order to do so, they are to set their minds (*phroneite*) on those matters and behave accordingly (3:1-2). The parallelism between the Greek terminology of setting one's mind and the scriptural behavioral "walking the way of God's law" is at its clearest in Rom 8:3-8:

> For God has done what the law, weakened by the flesh, could not do: sending his own Son in the likeness of sinful flesh and for sin, he condemned sin in the flesh, in order that the just requirement of *the law* might be fulfilled in us, who *walk* not according to the flesh but according to the Spirit. For those who are according to the flesh set their minds (*phronousin*) on the things of the flesh, but those who are according to the Spirit set their minds on the things of the Spirit. To set the mind (*to phronēma*) on the flesh is death, but to set the mind (*to phronēma*) on the Spirit is life and peace. For the mind that is set (*to phronēma*) on the flesh is hostile to God; it does not *submit to God's law*, indeed it cannot; and those who are in the flesh cannot please God.

However, the Colossians are not to be fooled by imagining that they are already in the heavens with Christ. Such life lies ahead and, for the time being, is "hidden" (Col 3:3). At the appointed time, Christ, in whom that life is hidden, will be revealed in his glory, and they will then share in that glory (v.4).

And in order to accede to such *life*, the Colossians must *put to death* their former way of life, which is summed up in idolatry (v.5). As is usual in a list of nouns, the first element sums up the rest of the elements in that list. These other elements function as different and multi-faceted expressions of that first element. The classic example is the list concerning the fruit of the Spirit in Galatians: "But the fruit of the Spirit is love, joy, peace, patience, kindness, goodness, faithfulness, gentleness, self-control." (5:22-23a) Notice how all nine elements are considered to be one fruit.[1] Conversely, although the opposite lengthy list is introduced as works of the flesh, still fornication (*porneia*;

---

[1] See my detailed comments in *Gal* 297-301.

harlotry) actually sums up all of them.² This understanding is corroborated in that *porneia* heads virtually all such lists (1 Cor 5:10, 11; 6:9; Eph 5:3, 5). Furthermore, *porneia* is singled out as the sin par excellence (1 Cor 6:15-19; Rev 17-19). The reason is that harlotry is the classic metaphoric expression of turning away from God to following other kings and their deities (see e.g. Ezek 16; 23; Hos 2). It is therefore the expression of idolatry, which is clear from the cases where harlotry (*porneia*) parallels idolatry (1 Cor 10:7-8; Rev 2:14, 20). This explains why, in Colossians 3:5, harlotry and its other expressions (impurity, passion, evil desire, and covetousness) are said to be namely idolatry. It is precisely by following the dictates of other deities, which was the life the Colossians "walked" (v.7), that will incur God's wrath (v.6), should they return to such life. Now that they pledged obedience to the scriptural God, they are to avoid their previous behavior (vv.8-9a). Put metaphorically, as was done in 2:11, they are to "put off the old kind of being with its practices" (3:9b) and "put on the new kind of being that is being renewed in knowledge after the image of its creator" (v.10). The terminology of v.10b (renewed in knowledge after the image of its creator) is a compact rendering of 1:9-10 concerning the Colossians' behavior[3] and 1:13-15 that speak of Christ as being their prime example.[4]

The combination of "renewed" and "creator" recalls the phrase "new creation" in Galatians 6:15, especially when one considers

---

[2] See my detailed comments in *Gal* 293-6.

[3] "And so, from the day we heard of it, we have not ceased to pray for you, asking that you may be filled with the knowledge of his will in all spiritual wisdom and understanding, to lead a life worthy of the Lord, fully pleasing to him, bearing fruit in every good work and increasing in the knowledge of God."

[4] "He has delivered us from the dominion of darkness and transferred us to the kingdom of his beloved Son, in whom we have redemption, the forgiveness of sins, and who is the image of the invisible God, the first-born of all creation."

that the root *kain*— (meaning "new") which is the basis of the adjective *anakainoumenon* (renewed) is a unique instance in Colossians. That Galatians was on the writer's mind is evident in that Galatians 3:27-28 functions as the blueprint for Colossians 3:10-11:

> For as many of you as were baptized into Christ have put on Christ. There is neither Jew nor Greek, there is neither slave nor free, there is no male and female; for you are all one in Christ Jesus. (Gal 3:27-28)

> ... and have put on the new being, which is being renewed in knowledge after the image of its creator. Here there cannot be Greek and Jew, circumcised and uncircumcised, barbarian, Scythian, slave, free man, but Christ is all, and in all. (Col 3:10-11)

The addition of "circumcised and uncircumcised" in Colossians can be explained in that, earlier, Paul spoke of the circumcision in Christ as being a "putting off" of that done in the flesh (2:11). The addition of barbarian and even the Scythian, the farthest barbarian from the perspective of the Roman empire, is intended to stress the full inclusiveness of God's household through the gospel. The Scythians were residing totally outside the boundaries of the Roman empire. Consequently, Paul was hinting to the inhabitants of Colossae, a mini-Rome, that the gospel message has already succeeded in an area where the mighty Romans have not yet set foot!

Putting on Christ is in no way a mystical experience. Rather, as Paul indicates to the Philippians (2:1-5), it consists of emulating Christ, their head, by putting up with one another graciously (compare Col 3:13 with Phil 2:3-5). Practically speaking, this means to don "entrails of mercy" (*splankhna oiktirmou*) in humility (*tapeinophrosynēn*; lowliness) (Col 3:12; compare with Phil 2:1 and 3). And since these are expressions of love (Col 3:14), Paul adds to the elements found in Philippians "kindness" (*khrēstotēta*), "meekness" (*prautēta*), and "patience" (*makrothymian*; forbearance) from the list expanding on "love" in Galatians 5:22-23. Love, which has been on Paul's mind since the beginning of the letter, is the "ligament" (*syndesmos*; link) of perfection (Col 3:14), that is to say, the "ligament" that binds "the whole body" (2:19)[5] together in perfection (*teleiotētos*), ensuring that "every man" would be "presented perfect (*teleion*)" before God on judgment day (1:28). Beyond that judgment, should the Colossians be found perfect in their love for the others, they will attain the prized peace of the Kingdom where all will be as "one body." Yet, even if they succeed in attaining that goal, they still ought to be thankful (3:15) since "God is at work in you, both to will and to work for his good pleasure" (Phil 2:13).

At this point, Paul wraps up his exhortation by reverting to what he started with, the gospel "word" carrying Christ to the Colossians.[6] He prays that that word "abide" among them richly whenever they share table fellowship in the house churches. At those gatherings they are to do their share in imparting the gospel wisdom by teaching and exhorting one another. The safest way to do so is to recite psalms. The primacy given to psalms is evident in 1 Corinthians 14 where Paul gives directives regarding the church gatherings: "What then, brethren? When

---

[5] Col 2:19 reads "… and not holding fast to the Head, from whom the whole body, nourished and knit together through its joints and ligaments (*syndesmōn*), grows with a growth that is from God."

[6] Compare *ho logos tou Khristou* (the word of Christ) to *rhēma Khristou* (the utterance [word] of Christ) in Rom 10:17 to speak of the gospel.

you come together, each one has a psalm (*psalmon*),[7] a teaching, a revelation, a tongue, or an interpretation, let all things be done for edification." (v.26) The four elements mentioned after "psalm" have been part of the lengthy discussion regarding edification (*oikodomēn*; 3, 4 [twice], 5, 12, 17): teaching (*didakhēn*; v.6), revelation (*apokalypsin*; v.6), tongue (*glōssan*; vv.5 [twice], 6, 9, 13, 14, 18, 19, 22, 23) and interpretation (*hermēneian*; vv.5, 13). Although "psalm" has not been part of the discussion, it suddenly appears in its conclusion (v.26) and no less than at the head of the list, and not as afterthought or an appendage. Psalms have the same place of honor in Colossians and Ephesians:

> Let the word of Christ dwell among you richly, teaching (*didaskontes*) and exhorting (*nouthetountes*) one another in all wisdom, singing (*adontes*) psalms and hymns and spiritual songs in your hearts to God as recognition of the (divine) grace (*en khariti*). And whatever you do, in word or deed, do everything in the name of the Lord Jesus, giving thanks to God the Father through him. (Col 3:16-17)

> ... but be filled with the Spirit, addressing (*lalountes*) one another in psalms and hymns and spiritual songs, singing (*adontes*) and making psalmody (*psallontes*) to the Lord with all your heart, always and for everything giving thanks in the name of our Lord Jesus Christ to God the Father. (Eph 5:18b-20)

It is my conviction that the psalms Paul is referring to here are the scriptural psalms contained in the Book of Psalms. The "teaching and exhorting with the word of Christ in all wisdom" of Colossians 3:16 is a carbon copy of what Paul wrote of his preaching Christ in 1:28: "whom [Christ] we proclaim, exhorting (*nouthetountes*) every man and teaching (*didaskontes*)

---

[7] RSV renders the Greek *psalmon* into "hymn."

every man in all wisdom." Thus, in Paul's absence, the Colossians are to sustain one another with Paul's gospel, which is confirmed in the use of the phrase "the word of Christ." The same thought is reflected in the parallel text in Ephesians where the verb *lalountes* (speaking), which usually refer to the apostolic teaching in Paul's epistles,[8] is used. Finally, the addition of *psallontes* (making psalmody) after *adontes* (singing) in Ephesians forms an *inclusio* with "psalms," underscoring the centrality of psalms as part of the overall conversation among the attendees in the house-church gatherings. This addition seems intended to sub-ordain "singing," cultic or otherwise, a feature of festive gatherings, to "psalmody" or "psalmodic singing." But why would the (communal) recitation of psalms by the believers ensure that the gospel teaching be maintained in the absence, or after the death, of the apostle? More specifically, how would the recitation of psalms function as another expression of the apostolic teaching (Col 3:16) unto the edification of the church (1 Cor 14:26)?

In actuality, Paul's exposition of the gospel is not only based on "the (Old Testament) holy scriptures" (Rom 1:1-2) but in fact follows the flow of the (Old Testament) scriptural story consigned in the Law and the Prophets. In my commentaries on Galatians and Romans, I have repeatedly shown this to be the case. On the other hand, my study of the Book of Psalms has evidenced that the structure of this book reflects that same scriptural story line. It is not an amalgamation of disconnected individual psalms; rather it is a total book sketching the story of Jerusalem and its temple with their collapse, followed by the prophetic hope of a new heavenly Jerusalem with its temple, not

---

[8] Rom 15:18; 1 Cor 2:6, 7, 13; 3:1; 9:8; 14 (passim); 2 Cor 2:17; 4;13; 11:17 [twice], 23; 12:19; 13:3; Eph 6:20; Phil 1:14; 1 Thess 2:2, 4, 16.

made by the hand of man, where the true worship consists in a psalmodic praise of God's universal kingship.⁹ Consequently, reciting the psalms as the liturgy of the heavenly Jerusalem, rather than as individual prayers for sundry occasions, will function as a reminder to those gathered at table fellowship in the house churches that they are citizens of that city rather than Rome (Phil 3:21; see also 1:27), or even Jerusalem for that matter (Gal 4:25-26).¹⁰ Instead of singing hymns to the deities or popular songs, the believers are to intone psalms of their heavenly citizenry. By the same token, those who are so gifted are encouraged to produce similar "hymns and spiritual songs," which function as a "gift of the spirit" on a par with the other gifts whose aim is to edify the church (1 Cor 14:26). My understanding is confirmed in Colossians 3:17 where the congregation members, whether they use the "word" of teaching or "work" with their hands as the deacons, actually join in Paul's apostolic ministry, whose ultimate function is to render thanksgiving to God the Father in the name of the Lord Jesus (1:12).

Vv. 18-25 ¹⁸Αἱ γυναῖκες, ὑποτάσσεσθε τοῖς ἀνδράσιν ὡς ἀνῆκεν ἐν κυρίῳ. ¹⁹ Οἱ ἄνδρες, ἀγαπᾶτε τὰς γυναῖκας καὶ μὴ πικραίνεσθε πρὸς αὐτάς. ²⁰ Τὰ τέκνα, ὑπακούετε τοῖς γονεῦσιν κατὰ πάντα, τοῦτο γὰρ εὐάρεστόν ἐστιν ἐν κυρίῳ. ²¹ Οἱ πατέρες, μὴ ἐρεθίζετε τὰ τέκνα ὑμῶν, ἵνα μὴ ἀθυμῶσιν. ²² Οἱ δοῦλοι, ὑπακούετε κατὰ πάντα τοῖς κατὰ σάρκα κυρίοις, μὴ ἐν ὀφθαλμοδουλίᾳ ὡς ἀνθρωπάρεσκοι, ἀλλ' ἐν ἁπλότητι καρδίας φοβούμενοι τὸν κύριον. ²³ ὃ ἐὰν ποιῆτε, ἐκ ψυχῆς ἐργάζεσθε ὡς τῷ κυρίῳ καὶ οὐκ ἀνθρώποις, ²⁴ εἰδότες ὅτι ἀπὸ κυρίου ἀπολήμψεσθε τὴν ἀνταπόδοσιν τῆς κληρονομίας. τῷ κυρίῳ Χριστῷ δουλεύετε· ²⁵ ὁ γὰρ ἀδικῶν κομίσεται ὃ ἠδίκησεν, καὶ οὐκ ἔστιν προσωπολημψία.

---

⁹ *OTI₃* 99-104.
¹⁰ See my comments on those verses in *C-Phil* and *Gal*.

V. 4:1 ¹Οἱ κύριοι, τὸ δίκαιον καὶ τὴν ἰσότητα τοῖς δούλοις παρέχεσθε, εἰδότες ὅτι καὶ ὑμεῖς ἔχετε κύριον ἐν οὐρανῷ.

¹⁸*Wives, be subject to your husbands, as is fitting in the Lord.* ¹⁹*Husbands, love your wives, and do not be harsh with them.* ²⁰*Children, obey your parents in everything, for this pleases the Lord.* ²¹*Fathers, do not provoke your children, lest they become discouraged.* ²²*Slaves, obey in everything those who are your earthly masters, not with eyeservice, as men-pleasers, but in singleness of heart, fearing the Lord.* ²³*Whatever your task, work heartily, as serving the Lord and not men,* ²⁴*knowing that from the Lord you will receive the inheritance as your reward; you are serving the Lord Christ.* ²⁵*For the wrongdoer will be paid back for the wrong he has done, and there is no partiality.*

⁴:¹*Masters, treat your slaves justly and fairly, knowing that you also have a Master in heaven.*

After having set the rules for the communal gatherings at table fellowship, Paul moves to the rules for everyday life, which is the real test for abiding by the primary rule of love that binds everybody together into the perfection (3:14) required by God (1:28; 4:12). And since Paul's interest in Colossians is essentially the house church and, by the same token, the Roman household, his rules governing mutual love are house rules that govern husbands and wives (3:18-19), parents and children (vv.20-21), and masters and slaves (3:22-4:1). Noticeable is that, in all three cases, the one under authority is addressed first, however, pressure is put on the one in the position of authority to remind him that just as Christ is "head of the body," he is the one ultimately responsible for the good or bad state of the household. That is why the entire passage ends by reminding the "lords" of the households—husbands, fathers, masters—that they will have to answer to *their* "heavenly lord" (4:1). Actually, the lordship of Christ controls the entire sets of relationships; in each case, his lordship is brought up as the point of reference in the attitude of subordination required of the subaltern (3:18, 20, 22-24).

In requesting that the wives be sub-ordained (*hypotassesthe*) to their husbands, Paul's intention is to maintain the "order" (*taxin*)[11] in the household daily life and, by extension, in the church gatherings held at the same household. Such order is necessary for the "word of the Lord" to be heard (Col 2:5; 1 Cor 14:4). The paterfamilias is the sole master and every household member, including the wife, is sub-ordained to him. She may well be his best confidant and even influence him greatly, but she may not contradict him publicly. That is why she is to be sub-ordained to her husband "as is befitting." However, Paul ups the ante by saying that it is even more befitting since ultimately the actual lord of the believing household is the Lord Christ himself (Col 3:24; 4:1); thus the ruling of the household has its source not in the husband, but in Christ, the only true representative of God the (ultimate) Father "from whom every *patria* (fatherhood; family) in heaven and on earth gets its name (and thus ultimately originates)" (Eph 3:15). Consequently, the husband's duty is simply to abide by the rule of love which requires him not to indulge and revel in his absolute authority in order to exercise *his* will. Rather, such rule of love summons him to "forbear his wife and, if she has a complaint against him, forgive her; as the Lord has been gracious to (*ekahrisato*; forgive) him" (Col 3:13), so he also must be gracious to his wife and thus not "embitter" (*pikrainesthe*) her by being harsh to her (v.19). In this way, through such love toward his wife, the husband will ensure the bond of perfection in his household (v.14).

---

[11] *hypotassesthe* and *taxin* are from the same root *tassō* (put in order) as is the verb *diatassomai* (ordain, set as rule) which Paul uses to refer to his instructions in all the churches (1 Cor 7:17).

The children are to obey their parents in everything. The reason given is that such is well pleasing (*evareston*) to the Lord. The finality of this reason is borne by that the "pleasing behavior" (*areskeian*) is ultimately toward the Lord *as judge* (1:9-11; see also Rom 12:1-2; 14:17-18). The importance of honoring one's parents is in fact the first commandment concerning conduct toward the others and, further, that one's own prosperity is bound to that respect for one's elders: "Honor your father and your mother, *that your days may be long in the earth* which the Lord your God gives you" (Ex 20:12); "Honor your father and your mother, as the Lord your God commanded you; *that your days may be prolonged, and that it may go well with you, in the earth* which the Lord your God gives you." (Deut 5:16) On the other hand, since parents are not the Lord, they are not to judge their children, nor even to provoke (*erethizete*) them through undue harshness, so that the children not be discouraged on the difficult path of obedience.

The same applies to the slaves who are also household children. They are to obey their earthly masters in everything and be genuine in their efforts and not feign pleasing their masters, even though these can be fooled. The slaves are to obey their masters with simplicity of heart, that is to say, in earnest, out of fear for the Lord whom they ultimately are to please and who cannot be mocked (Gal 6:7). They are to fulfill their duty as though it is toward the Lord, knowing that they are looking for the inheritance of the Kingdom that comes from him, and not for the earthly inheritance of their household master. After all, they are in the service of Christ the Lord, and they will undergo God's impartial judgment against any unjust behavior. On the other hand, the masters (*kyrioi*; lords) are to behave *lordly*, securing all justice and equity (fairness) for their slaves. The reason is that they too are under the judgment of the Lord in heaven whence he is coming to judge all, masters as well as slaves.

It is clear that the pressure is on the *paterfamilias* who is to secure that his household be the household of God. When hearing the text in the original Greek, the intention is unmistakable since the term for parents in Colossians 3:21 is *pateres* (literally, fathers). Thus the three sets of "seniors" –the husbands (men; v.19), the "fathers" (v.21) and the masters (lords; 4:1)—are all titles that apply to the *paterfamilias*. Just as God's Christ is the ultimate manager and thus responsible for the well-being of the world, so the Roman patrician ultimately is accountable for making the members of his household "citizens of God's kingdom by leading a life worthy of the gospel's instructions" (Phil 1:27). His compass is the continual thought that he has a master in heaven (Col 4:1b).

Chapter 4

Vv. 2-6 ² Τῇ προσευχῇ προσκαρτερεῖτε, γρηγοροῦντες ἐν αὐτῇ ἐν εὐχαριστίᾳ, ³ προσευχόμενοι ἅμα καὶ περὶ ἡμῶν, ἵνα ὁ θεὸς ἀνοίξῃ ἡμῖν θύραν τοῦ λόγου λαλῆσαι τὸ μυστήριον τοῦ Χριστοῦ, δι' ὃ καὶ δέδεμαι, ⁴ ἵνα φανερώσω αὐτὸ ὡς δεῖ με λαλῆσαι. ⁵ Ἐν σοφίᾳ περιπατεῖτε πρὸς τοὺς ἔξω τὸν καιρὸν ἐξαγοραζόμενοι. ⁶ ὁ λόγος ὑμῶν πάντοτε ἐν χάριτι, ἅλατι ἠρτυμένος, εἰδέναι πῶς δεῖ ὑμᾶς ἑνὶ ἑκάστῳ ἀποκρίνεσθαι.

> ²*Continue steadfastly in prayer, being watchful in it with thanksgiving;* ³*and pray for us also, that God may open to us a door for the word, to declare the mystery of Christ, on account of which I am in prison,* ⁴*that I may make it clear, as I ought to speak.* ⁵*Conduct yourselves wisely toward outsiders, making the most of the time.* ⁶*Let your speech always be gracious, seasoned with salt, so that you may know how you ought to answer every one.*

In the following verses that end his exhortation Paul invites the citizens of Colossae to realize that the world does not revolve around their local house churches. Rather, through Paul their apostle, they are part of a larger community of believers that goes even beyond Rome and extends over the entire empire. Just as he asks the Romans to be "constant in prayer" (*tē prosevkhē proskarterountes*; Rom 12:12c), here also Paul summons the Colossians to "continue steadfastly in prayer" (*proskartereite tē prosevkhē*; Col 4:2a). The prayer he is referring to is specifically that of thanksgiving at table fellowship where the house church gathers around the word of Paul, their high priest. They are to pray that God will open new doors for him to continue preaching the gospel throughout the Roman empire (see also Rom 15:18-29). In the meantime, they are to "walk" according to the wisdom of the gospel preached to them by Paul (Col 4:5;

see 1:9-10), taking every opportunity to witness to the outsiders that the true wisdom sought after by the Greco-Romans actually lies in God's commandments and not in vain philosophical endeavors (2:8). To the extent to which they use that same "word" (of the gospel) of grace to answer the inquiries of the outsiders, the daily lives of those outsiders will be seasoned with true meaning. Thus, the Colossians will be the "salt of the (Roman) earth" around them (Mt 5:13; see also Mk 9:50; Lk 14:34).

Vv. 7-18 ⁷ Τὰ κατ' ἐμὲ πάντα γνωρίσει ὑμῖν Τύχικος ὁ ἀγαπητὸς ἀδελφὸς καὶ πιστὸς διάκονος καὶ σύνδουλος ἐν κυρίῳ, ⁸ ὃν ἔπεμψα πρὸς ὑμᾶς εἰς αὐτὸ τοῦτο, ἵνα γνῶτε τὰ περὶ ἡμῶν καὶ παρακαλέσῃ τὰς καρδίας ὑμῶν, ⁹ σὺν Ὀνησίμῳ τῷ πιστῷ καὶ ἀγαπητῷ ἀδελφῷ, ὅς ἐστιν ἐξ ὑμῶν· πάντα ὑμῖν γνωρίσουσιν τὰ ὧδε. ¹⁰ Ἀσπάζεται ὑμᾶς Ἀρίσταρχος ὁ συναιχμάλωτός μου καὶ Μᾶρκος ὁ ἀνεψιὸς Βαρναβᾶ (περὶ οὗ ἐλάβετε ἐντολάς, ἐὰν ἔλθῃ πρὸς ὑμᾶς, δέξασθε αὐτόν) ¹¹ καὶ Ἰησοῦς ὁ λεγόμενος Ἰοῦστος, οἱ ὄντες ἐκ περιτομῆς, οὗτοι μόνοι συνεργοὶ εἰς τὴν βασιλείαν τοῦ θεοῦ, οἵτινες ἐγενήθησάν μοι παρηγορία. ¹² ἀσπάζεται ὑμᾶς Ἐπαφρᾶς ὁ ἐξ ὑμῶν, δοῦλος Χριστοῦ [Ἰησοῦ], πάντοτε ἀγωνιζόμενος ὑπὲρ ὑμῶν ἐν ταῖς προσευχαῖς, ἵνα σταθῆτε τέλειοι καὶ πεπληροφορημένοι ἐν παντὶ θελήματι τοῦ θεοῦ. ¹³ μαρτυρῶ γὰρ αὐτῷ ὅτι ἔχει πολὺν πόνον ὑπὲρ ὑμῶν καὶ τῶν ἐν Λαοδικείᾳ καὶ τῶν ἐν Ἱεραπόλει. ¹⁴ ἀσπάζεται ὑμᾶς Λουκᾶς ὁ ἰατρὸς ὁ ἀγαπητὸς καὶ Δημᾶς. ¹⁵ Ἀσπάσασθε τοὺς ἐν Λαοδικείᾳ ἀδελφοὺς καὶ Νύμφαν καὶ τὴν κατ' οἶκον αὐτῆς ἐκκλησίαν. ¹⁶ καὶ ὅταν ἀναγνωσθῇ παρ' ὑμῖν ἡ ἐπιστολή, ποιήσατε ἵνα καὶ ἐν τῇ Λαοδικέων ἐκκλησίᾳ ἀναγνωσθῇ, καὶ τὴν ἐκ Λαοδικείας ἵνα καὶ ὑμεῖς ἀναγνῶτε. ¹⁷ καὶ εἴπατε Ἀρχίππῳ· Βλέπε τὴν διακονίαν ἣν παρέλαβες ἐν κυρίῳ, ἵνα αὐτὴν πληροῖς. ¹⁸ Ὁ ἀσπασμὸς τῇ ἐμῇ χειρὶ Παύλου. μνημονεύετέ μου τῶν δεσμῶν. ἡ χάρις μεθ' ὑμῶν.

⁷*Tychicus will tell you all about my affairs; he is a beloved brother and faithful minister and fellow servant in the Lord. ⁸I have sent him*

to you for this very purpose, that you may know how we are and that he may encourage your hearts, ⁹and with him Onesimus, the faithful and beloved brother, who is one of yourselves. They will tell you of everything that has taken place here. ¹⁰Aristarchus my fellow prisoner greets you, and Mark the cousin of Barnabas (concerning whom you have received instructions—if he comes to you, receive him), ¹¹and Jesus who is called Justus. These are the only men of the circumcision among my fellow workers for the kingdom of God, and they have been a comfort to me. ¹²Epaphras, who is one of yourselves, a servant of Christ Jesus, greets you, always remembering you earnestly in his prayers, that you may stand mature and fully assured in all the will of God. ¹³For I bear him witness that he has worked hard for you and for those in Laodicea and in Hierapolis. ¹⁴Luke the beloved physician and Demas greet you. ¹⁵Give my greetings to the brethren at Laodicea, and to Nympha and the church in her house. ¹⁶And when this letter has been read among you, have it read also in the church of the Laodiceans; and see that you read also the letter from Laodicea. ¹⁷And say to Archippus, "See that you fulfil the ministry which you have received in the Lord." ¹⁸I, Paul, write this greeting with my own hand. Remember my fetters. Grace be with you.

Through his final greetings the Apostle is leaving the Colossian church and, via it, all the churches of the province Asia and thus of the Roman empire at large, in the hands of God, after his own demise by execution which he alludes to in the use of *dedemai* (I am imprisoned; Col 4:3). In order to console the Colossians, he is sending them Tychicus, whose name (*Tykhikos*) means "fortuitous, chosen by chance" and thus is equivalent to Epaphras, one of their own co-citizens, who is imprisoned with Paul. Put otherwise, Paul is telling the Colossians that God will not leave their church bereft even after the eventual demise of Epaphras, their deacon. God will raise another minister (*diakonos*) of his choice, namely Tychicus, who will be as faithful as Epaphras (1:7). Moreover, Tychicus is a beloved brother to

Paul and a faithful minister. Finally and most importantly, Tychicus is of the value of Timothy in that he, like Epaphras before him (Col 1:9; see also 4:12), is a fellow-slave of Paul (4:7; compare with Phil 1:1). So the Colossians are not to worry; God will take care of them through whomever he chooses as ministers of the church in Colossae. These ministers, whoever they might "fortuitously" be, will be factually Paul's emissaries to encourage (*parakalesē*; exhort, console) the Colossians' hearts (Col 4:8b) with the word of his gospel. In addition, there is Onesimus, the other beloved and faithful brother (v.9a), whose name (*Onēsimos*) means "helpful, profitable." He will have the same function as Tychicus (v.9c [they both *will tell you all* that has taken place here]; compare with v.7a [Tychicus *will tell you all that concerns me*]). However, just as Epaphras (v.12), Onesimus is one of the Colossians (v.9b). Consequently, God definitely will not let go of the Colossians in that, instead of the one Epaphras, he will raise two in his place to lead the Colossian church.

Actually, the future of the Colossian church together with all the churches of the Roman province Asia looks bright in that the main Jewish leaders are now at one regarding the gospel championed by Paul. This is what transpires from the symbolic terminology of v. 10. The numeral three indicates the fullness of witness[1] and thus reflects the certainty of the reality advocated. By including three leaders of the circumcision in the one greeting (notice the singular *aspazetai* [greets] only once in conjunction with Aristarchus, the first named in the series) Paul is underlining their oneness in thought. The first of the three is named Aristarchus, from the Greek *Aristarkhos* meaning

---

[1] Am 4:8; Mt 18:16, 20; 1 Cor 14:29; 2 Cor 13:1; 1 Tim 5:19; Heb 10:28. See also my comments on the numeral three in *NTI₃* 22-25.

"excellent in leadership." Moreover, he is Paul's "fellow prisoner" (*synaikhmalōtos*). The Greek *synaikhmalōtos* actually means "war captive" and entails deportation and exile. Thus, Aristarchus is intended to be someone who, like Paul, is a Jewish Roman citizen of the diaspora. He may even be a cryptic reference to Paul himself.

The second name in the series is Mark, from the Latin name *Marcus* meaning "hammer."[2] His connection with Barnabas makes him clearly the John Mark of Acts who vacillated regarding the apostolic mission to the Gentiles and became the reason behind the split between Paul and Barnabas (Acts 15:37-40). To show that Mark has been rehabilitated, Paul has to give specific instructions, actually "command(ment)s" (*entolas*), that the Colossians receive him (Col 4:10) as one of the leaders in the Pauline camp.

More important than his connection with Barnabas is Mark's relationship with Peter (Acts 12:11-14); the closeness of this relationship is evidenced in that Peter refers to Mark as his "son" (1 Pet 5:13). By rehabilitating Mark, the Pauline school was actually eyeing to rehabilitate Peter, Paul's apostolic counterpart (Gal 2:7-8). Colossians was the charter of the Pauline school headquartered in Ephesus, the capital of the province Asia.[3] Upon joining that school, Mark wrote his Gospel in which the main anti-hero is Peter, who keeps faltering until the end, and then is offered the chance to redeem himself by starting anew in the Galilee of the nations (Mk 14:28; 16:7). In essence, 2 Peter seems to function as the expression of Peter's repentance and rehabilitation after having betrayed the cause of the gospel in

---

[2] See on this matter *NTI₄* 57-8.
[3] *NTI₁* 105 and *NTI₄* 60-64.

Antioch (Gal 2:11-14): "So also our beloved brother Paul wrote to you according to the wisdom given him, speaking of this as he does in *all his letters*. There are some things in them hard to understand, which the ignorant and unstable twist to their own destruction, as they do *the other scriptures*." (2 Pet 3:15b-16). Thus by including the rehabilitated Mark next to Aristarchus in the triad of the Jewish diaspora leadership, Paul, in Colossians, was inviting the churches of Asia to accept the Gospel of Mark as the official "gospel of Jesus the Christ" (Mk 1:1).[4]

My reading is corroborated in that the third person of that triad is none other than Jesus Christ himself. Indeed, except for the two instances where Jesus is Joshua, son of Nun (Acts 7:45; Heb 4:8)[5] and a third instance of a Jesus/Joshua in the Lukan genealogy of Jesus Christ (Lk 3:29), all other occurrences of Jesus refer to the Lord Jesus Christ. It would then be very strange if the "Jesus" here would be just simply a person by that name. Such is rendered virtually impossible due to the addition "who is called Justus (*Ioustos*)." The Greek is merely the transliteration of the Latin *Justus* which means "the just one, the righteous one." This is how the servant of the Lord is presented in Isaiah 53:10-12, the passage behind Colossians 1:14-20. That the author had in mind that passage from the beginning of the letter is evidenced in the use of the phrase "for the kingdom of God (*eis tēn basileian tou Theou*)" (4:11) that is reminiscent of "to (for) the kingdom of the Son of his love (of his beloved Son) (*eis tēn basileian tou hyiou tēs agapēs avtou*)" (1:13), which introduces vv.14-20.[6] We shall attain the Kingdom through the

---

[4] Regarding Colossians as being the charter of the Pauline school see *NTI₁* 105. Regarding Mark being a more systematic charter see *NTI₁* 119-20.
[5] The LXX uses *Iēsous* for the Hebrew *yehošuaʻ*.
[6] These are the only two instances of *basileian* (kingdom), actually of the root *basil*— (reign) in the entire letter.

righteousness that Jesus Christ has bestowed upon us. This is precisely *the* gospel that Peter and Paul had committed themselves to at the Jerusalem meeting (Gal 2:7-8), which is now being carried by Paul and Mark, his "fellow worker" (Col 4:11). "Fellow worker" is a term Paul uses to speak of his counterparts or helpers in the gospel preaching.[7] All of this is Paul's way to assure the Colossians that all is well in spite of what appears to be a small number of believers committed to the gospel cause. What matters, ultimately, is that the few are from among his and Peter's followers and are working together with God's Christ.

Corresponding to the fullness on the part of the circumcision expressed in the number three, Paul mentions a similar number from among his Gentile following. The first among these is Epaphras (1:7) who is introduced here as "one of yourselves" (4:12) and thus a Gentile. However, his function here has changed from someone who reports to Paul about the Colossians' abiding by the rule of love (1:8) to someone who "prays" on their behalf, as Paul does at the beginning of the letter (1:3-6, 9-10), that they may continue on that path (4:12). Put otherwise, Epaphras is put in the position of "high priest," which indicates that Paul is introducing him as his "heir" after the Apostle's eventual demise. Epaphras' "apostolic" status is further evidenced in Paul's referring to him as "having (shown) much painful toil (*ponon*) for your sake" (4:13a). This unique instance of *ponos* in the Pauline corpus is reminiscent of the apostolic *kopos* (toil);[8] whereas the latter connotes the effort exerted, the former entails physical pain along with that effort. The reason behind this choice of wording is that Epaphras is said to have

---

[7] Rom 16:3, 9, 21; 1 Cor 3:9; 16:16; 2 Cor 8:23; Phil 2:25; 4:3; 1 Thess 3:2; Philem 1, 24.
[8] 1 Cor 3:8; 15:38; 2 Cor 6:5; 10:15; 11:23, 27; 1 Thess 3:5; 2 Thess 3:8.

toiled also for the sake of the Laodiceans and Hierapolitans (v.13b).

Laodicea and the Laodiceans are mentioned three more times (vv.15-16), but what is unexpected is the addition, alongside Laodicea, of Hierapolis (v.13), a unique instance in the New Testament. Hierapolis means "holy city" and is thus an oblique reference to the heavenly Jerusalem. Thus, Epaphras, after Paul, will be the "high priest" of the heavenly Jerusalem and will challenge the citizens of Colossae to emulate the citizens of God's heavenly city. This is similar to what Paul requested of the Philippians (1:27; 3:20). What makes the metaphoric language even more powerful is that Laodicea means "the judgment of the people (by God)." Consequently, Paul is putting pressure on Epaphras to help his co-citizens choose the way of life (Hierapolis) over that of judgment and eventual condemnation (Laodicea).[9] This in turn explains why his labor is referred to as *ponos* instead of the more common *kopos*. Indeed, *ponos* occurs three more times in the New Testament to speak either of the sufferings linked to divine judgment (Rev 16:10 and 11) or of the lack of such suffering for those who end in the new Jerusalem (21:4). Epaphras is to take the duty of apostleship so seriously, not only with all the toil it entails, but also even the possible suffering, in order to save his co-citizens in Colossae from the eventual eternal suffering.

Besides Epaphras in the triad of leadership representing the Gentiles we hear of Luke and Demas.[10] These two names are also symbolic in that they reflect the gospel preached to the entire citizenry, thus expanding the mission of Epaphras beyond the

---

[9] See my comments on Bethany and Bethphage in Mk 11:1 as being two possibilities (options, choices) in *NTI₁* 202-3.
[10] The Greek *Epaphras, Loukas,* and *Dēmas* have the same ending.

province Asia to the entire Roman empire. The Greek *Loukas* (Luke) is the rendering of the Latin *Lucius* or *Lucianus*, a person that enlightens others, and the name *Dēmas* is from the Greek *dēmos* meaning people, (common) crowd. Taken in combination, the two names symbolize the message of the gospel that carries the light of the Law and its teaching to the Gentiles (Rom 2:17-20). This reading is supported by the fact that Luke is qualified by *iatros*, meaning the one who heals those in need of that healing. In the Gospels, Christ's teaching is often cast as a healing.[11] More apropos, in Luke, Christ the teacher refers to himself in a parabolic statement as a "physician" (*iatre*; 4:23). Moreover, the highest incidence of the verb *iaomai* (heal), from the same root as *iatros*, is found in Luke among the Gospels[12] and the noun *iasis* (healing) from the same root, occurs only in Luke-Acts (Lk 13:32; 4:22, 30). The centrality of this symbolism is corroborated in that, among the Evangelists, only Luke speaks of God's household as a *therapeia* (house of healing, healing institution; 12:42), and explicates Jesus' teaching about the kingdom of God as being a *therapeia* (healing) unto those who need it (9:11).[13]

What is more striking about each triad of names is that the names in each set have the same ending in Greek: —*os* ("us" in English) in the first and —*as* in the second. This seems to be intended, especially in view of the fact that the original Greek *Epaphroditos*, found in Philippians 2:25 and 4:18, has been

---

[11] Mt 4:23; 9:35; 10:1, 7-8; 13:14-15; Mk 6:2-5, 6a-13; Lk 4:14-30; 6:6-10; 9:1-2, 6, 11; 10:9; 13:10-12.

[12] Eleven times in Lk (+ 4 times in Acts) compared to thrice in Mt (+ once in a quotation from Is 6:10 in Mt 13:15), once in Mk, and twice in Jn (+ once in the same Isaianic quotation Jn 12:40).

[13] The latter understanding is found also in Rev 22:2 where the leaves of the tree of life in the heavenly Jerusalem are said to be "for the healing (*eis therapeian*) of the nations."

contracted into *Epaphras* in both Colossians (1:7; 4:12) and Philemon (23) where mention is made of Luke (Col 4:14; Philem 24) and also Mark (Col 4:10; Philem 24), together with Aristarchus (Col 4:10; Philem 24), Demas (Col 4:14; Philem 24), and Jesus Christ (Col 4:10; Philem 23). Thus, the contraction was made in order to make *Epaphras* correspond to *Loukas*. "Luke the physician" here ingeniously references the literary work Luke–Acts, written as the message to enlighten the people; Demas is representative of the Gentiles of the Roman empire. Epaphras in the letter functions as Paul's "heir" and "Luke" as the *writer* of Epaphras' Pauline teaching.

If the second triad is an intentional cluster, then most probably the first is also, especially that the ending —*os* appears in the added epithet *Ioustos* (Justus in English), rather than in the third name *Iēsous* (Col 4:11).[14] Reading then the first triad along the lines of the second, Aristarchus, "another" Paul or a stand-in for him,[15] would correspond to Epaphras in the second triad as the carrier of the Pauline "oral" teaching, whereas Mark would be the "author" who laid down this teaching in a written document. Jesus would consequently be the subject of that writing, which is precisely borne out in its title "(beginning of) the gospel of Jesus the Christ, the Son of God" (Mk 1:1), as I indicated earlier. Thus, Colossians 4:10-14 looks like an official endorsement by the Pauline school of the first two Gospels, Mark and Luke(-Acts), as reflecting Paul's legacy to the Gentiles as well as the Jews.

---

[14] *Ioustos* was added with the intention to create assonance between the endings within the triad and functions similarly to the contracted *Epaphras* in the second. The writer could have chosen *Khristos* over *Iēsous* to take care of the assonance in a simpler manner except for the fact that *Khristos* is not a personal name whereas *Iēsous* is.

[15] See my comments earlier on Col 4:10.

Having mentioned Demas, representative of the inhabitants of the Roman empire, the author reiterates what he wrote in the previous verse (Col 4:13) concerning the oneness of all the Pauline churches by asking the Colossians to greet the "brethren" in Laodicea and, more specifically, the church community headed by Nympha in her home (v.15); Nympha, meaning "bride," is a classic metaphor used to speak of the church in the Pauline corpus (2 Cor 11:2; Eph 5:25-32; see also 1 Cor 5:15-18). And what actually ensures the oneness among the churches is that the same apostolic word addressed to one of them applies also to the others (Col 4:16; see also Rev 2-3). So Paul asks that this letter be read in Laodicea and that the Colossians hear the letter from Laodicea. Doing so endorses the Pauline correspondence as a scriptural canon to be read in all the churches, an action that is iterated in 2 Peter 3:15-18. More specifically, Colossians 4:10-16 is actually *establishing* the blue print of a New Testament canon: Gospels, Acts, and a Pauline corpus.

This understanding is supported by the concluding verse: "And say to Archippus, 'See that you fulfil (*plērois*) the (table) ministry (*diakonian*) which you have received (*parelabes*) in the Lord (*en kyriō*).'" (v.17) This terminology is similar to that describing Paul's apostolic mission in 2:24-25.[16] Moreover, not only did Paul "receive" (*parelabon*) the gospel (1 Cor 15:3; Gal 1:12), but he did so in conjunction with the fellowship meal (For I received [*parelabon*] from the Lord [*apo tou kyriou*]; 1 Cor 11:11:23a). Thus, it is as though Archippus is summoned to "complete in his flesh what would still be lacking in Paul's endeavor for the sake

---

[16] "Now I rejoice in my sufferings for your sake, and in my flesh I complete (*antanaplērō*) what is lacking in Christ's afflictions for the sake of his body, that is, the church, of which I became a minister (*diakonos*) according to the divine office which was given to me for you, to complete (*plērōsai*) the word of God."

of the gospel" at the latter's death. Such is to be expected since, in the only other instance where he is mentioned (Philem 2), the "deacon" Archippus is heading Philemon and Apphia's house church as Paul's "fellow soldier," a title which occurs only one other time in the New Testament, and that in conjunction with Paul's "heir" Epaphroditus (Phil 2:25) who parallels the "deacon" Epaphras (Col 1:7).[17] On the other hand, the only two instances of "fellow prisoner" in the New Testament appear with Epaphras in Philemon 23 and Aristarchus (from the same root *arkh*— as Archippus and having the same connotation of rich and powerful) in Col 4:10. Consequently, in Colossians, Archippus would function as the "heir" after Aristarchus, just as Epaphroditus is Paul's heir after Timothy in Philippians.[18]

Can one say more about the choice of the name Archippus? While Archippus (*Arkhippos*) shares the root *arkhē* with Aristarchus (*Aristarkhos*), it also shares the root *(h)ippos* (horse) with Philip (*Philippos*). Actually Archippus and Philip have practically the same meaning: master (or tamer) of horses and lover of horses. Philip brings to mind his son Alexander, especially in conjunction with the latter's taming of the horse Bucephalus that became his personal mount throughout his conquest of Asia. Repeatedly in my discussion of the New Testament literature I have argued that the Pauline school cast the gospel itinerary as countering Alexander's and presented itself even more successful, in that Rome, the conqueror of Alexander's domain, submitted to the call of the scriptural God. Further, "the gospel of peace" succeeded without shedding blood, its armor being mainly defensive with the sole offensive instrument being "the sword of the Spirit, which is the *word* of

---

[17] See earlier on the sameness of Epaphroditus and Epaphras.
[18] See my discussion in *C-Phil* 140-2.

God" (Eph 6:13-16). This, in turn, may well have been behind the choice of the image of the white horse and its rider in conjunction with the gospel of salvation in Revelation (6:2; 19:11-21). Such hypothesis stands to reason given the parallelism mentioned above between Colossians 4:16 and Revelation 2-3 regarding letters addressed to individual churches being read authoritatively in other churches.

The last verse of the epistle supports my understanding that the New Testament canon was an internal phenomenon produced by that literature itself and not imposed on it by an external decision. The seed of the entire process was planted in the first New Testament document, the letter to the churches of Galatia. Not only was that letter addressed to a cluster of churches in one province or region, but it was sealed as scripture written "by the hand" (*tē kheiri*) of God's plenipotentiary emissary (Gal 6:11), just as the Law, the foundation of the Old Testament scripture, was handed down "at the hand" (*en kheiri*; through [RSV]) of an intermediary, Moses (3:19). Furthermore, the letter referred to itself as "canon" (*kanōn*; rule, 6:16). Thus, Colossians 4:10-16 is upholding a tradition already extant in Galatians.

Colossians 4:18 makes sense only when it is read along the same lines and in conjunction with the entire Pauline corpus of letters to churches (Romans through 2 Thessalonians) as a cluster, which confirms my thesis that those letters were written by the same school, if not concomitantly.[19] Indeed, the phrase "The greeting with my own hand, Paul" (*Ho aspasmos tē emē kheiri Pavlou*) is found at the end of 1 Corinthians (16:21), Colossians (4:18) and 2 Thessalonians (3:17). If one factors

---

[19] See *NTI₄* 70-80.

Galatians 6:11 (See with what large letters I am writing to you with my own hand [*tē emē kheiri*]), then this "personal signature" authenticates each cluster of two letters: Romans and 1 Corinthians, 2 Corinthians and Galatians, 1 and 2 Thessalonians. The oddity is the exception of Ephesians, Philippians, and Colossians. This oddity is explained in the addition "remember my fetters (*desmōn*; chains)" after "The greeting with my own hand, Paul" (Col 4:18). Those three letters, known as the captivity epistles, are the only ones among the nine letters to churches which account for the all the words of the root *desm*— (chaining, fettering).[20] On the other hand, the entire cluster of the nine letters to churches is sealed in 2 Thessalonians 3:17 which reads: "I, Paul, write this greeting with my own hand, Paul. *This is the mark (*sēmeion*; sign) in every letter of mine; it is the way (thus) I write.*"

Finally, we have the usual ending where Paul wishes to his hearers that they remain in the "grace" until they attain the "peace" at the end of the road (Col 1:2b). Having begun by wishing them grace and peace, Paul bids them farewell with the grace in which they now stand (Rom 5:2) with the hope that, should they continue on this "way," they shall attain salvation and the promised peace of the Kingdom (5:1-11).

---

[20] Eph 3:1; 4:1, 3; Phil 1:7, 13, 14, 17; Col 2:19; 3:14; 4:18.

Part II

Philemon

Chapter 5

Vv. 1-3 ¹Παῦλος δέσμιος Χριστοῦ Ἰησοῦ καὶ Τιμόθεος ὁ ἀδελφὸς Φιλήμονι τῷ ἀγαπητῷ καὶ συνεργῷ ἡμῶν ² καὶ Ἀπφίᾳ τῇ ἀδελφῇ καὶ Ἀρχίππῳ τῷ συστρατιώτῃ ἡμῶν καὶ τῇ κατ' οἶκόν σου ἐκκλησίᾳ, ³ χάρις ὑμῖν καὶ εἰρήνη ἀπὸ θεοῦ πατρὸς ἡμῶν καὶ κυρίου Ἰησοῦ Χριστοῦ.

> ¹*Paul, a prisoner for Christ Jesus, and Timothy our brother, To Philemon our beloved fellow worker* ²*and Apphia our sister and Archippus our fellow soldier, and the church in your house:* ³*Grace to you and peace from God our Father and the Lord Jesus Christ.*

Philemon is the only Pauline epistle where Paul introduces himself as a "prisoner" (*desmios*; chained) of the Christ Jesus (v.1); Philippians is the only letter where Paul introduces himself and Timothy as "slaves" (*douloi*) of the same Jesus (1:1). In my commentary on Philippians I show how this introduction plays a central role in the argument of the letter: not only Paul but even Jesus Christ himself is the "slave" of God (2:7). Consequently, the Philippians are in no better position and should be acting in full obedience to God (vv.12-13). Here in Philemon, the "chaining in prison" forms the crimson thread of the epistle: four occurrences of the root *desm—* in a mere 25 verses.[1] Actually, the "chaining" controls the letter both formally and materially. Just as Paul the "slave" is the one who nevertheless speaks with authority in Philippians, here also the "chained" Paul has the upper hand in relation to Philemon, the free Roman patrician. The "chaining" is particularly functional in Paul's actual argument concerning the reception due Onesimus by Philemon (Philem 10, 14).

---

[1] Vv.1, 9, 10, 13.

The inclusion of Timothy as co-author in Philemon, as in Colossians, without further mention of him in the body of the letter is to be explained against the fact that he is to be Paul's successor and later will become the bishop of Ephesus (1 Tim 1:3; 4:13-16), the capital of the Roman province Asia where the city of Colossae lay.

The addressees are Philemon, Apphia, and Archippus. The main personage is obviously Philemon who is the head of his house church. His name is from the root *phil*— connoting brotherly or friendly love; thus Philemon is the one who provides the necessary care for the community life within his household. By the same token, he is bound by such love, as Paul will make clear later in the letter: Philemon will be called upon, indeed challenged, to live up to his name. However, Paul is already putting on the pressure through the two epithets with which he qualifies Philemon. He is Paul's co-worker and thus equally "bound" (*desmios*), before anything else, by the rules of the gospel Paul is preaching. Further, Philemon became Paul's co-worker because he is "beloved," that is, because he was loved first. This teaching, a staple of the Pauline gospel (Rom 5:8; 1 Cor 8:3; Gal 2:20; 4:9), is immortalized in the statement "We love, because he first loved us" (1 Jn 4:19). So, when Philemon will be summoned to treat Onesimus mercifully, that action actually amounts to repaying his due to Paul, the one who put him on the gospel path (Philem 19b), and through Paul to God himself.

The second person named in the greeting is Apphia, who is introduced as "sister." Per se, this appellation indicates that the person is a believer, someone who accepted the gospel and thus is a member of the church community. However, in the actual context, it puts Apphia on an equal footing with Timothy "the brother," clearly indicating that she is in a position of leadership in Philemon's house church; most probably, she is either his wife or his sister. Her name brings to mind the Via Appia, a most important Roman road that linked Rome to Brundisium (actual Brindisi), a major port city in southeastern Italy and the "gate" of Rome to the East. That road served to carry the Roman armies to the eastern parts of the empire and, at the same time, to bring the subjugated enemies in the East back to Rome as slaves.[2]

Also included in the greeting is Archippus, a "fellow soldier." As I explained in Colossians, Archippus is representative of a member of the Roman cavalry. Thus he is someone who toils for the sake of the gospel, just as does Epaphroditus, another fellow soldier of Paul (Phil 2:25). The resulting impression is that Paul, the "chained prisoner" of the Roman authorities, is setting up a bastion of counterattack against the power of Rome in one of the most important Roman provinces of the East. This is not done through the authority of the sword, but through a house church that is led by love (Philemon), where the soldiers (the like of Archippus) open the way (Apphia) for conquest through the gospel of love for all. This way leads to the Jerusalem above, the city of God and his slaughtered Lamb (Rev 21:22; 22:3), instead of Rome, Caesar's city. This teaching, which is also reflected in Colossians,[3] is magisterially summed up in the letter addressed to Ephesus, the capital of the province Asia, where Paul pits the gospel of peace, whose panoply is essentially defensive, against the aggressive behavior of Rome:

---

[2] The choice of Apphia over Appia may have been intended to make the name consonant with the Hebrew verb *'aphah* which means "bake." If so, then the secondary connotation would have been that Apphia was the mistress of the house where the church table fellowship took place.

[3] See earlier my comments on Archippus in Col 4:17.

Finally, be strong in the Lord and in the strength of his might. Put on the whole armor of God, that you may be able to stand against the wiles of the devil. For we are not contending against flesh and blood, but against the principalities, against the powers, against the world rulers of this present darkness, against the spiritual hosts of wickedness in the heavenly places. Therefore take the whole armor of God, that you may be able to withstand in the evil day, and having done all, to stand. Stand therefore, having girded your loins with truth, and having put on the breastplate of righteousness, and having shod your feet with the equipment of the gospel of peace; besides all these, taking the shield of faith, with which you can quench all the flaming darts of the evil one. And take the helmet of salvation, and the sword of the Spirit, which is the word of God. (Eph 6:10-17)

As usual, Paul ends his salutation with the wish of grace, which is the starting point of God's "way," and the hope of divine peace, which will materialize in God's city.[4]

Vv. 4-7 ⁴Εὐχαριστῶ τῷ θεῷ μου πάντοτε μνείαν σου ποιούμενος ἐπὶ τῶν προσευχῶν μου, ⁵ ἀκούων σου τὴν ἀγάπην καὶ τὴν πίστιν, ἣν ἔχεις πρὸς τὸν κύριον Ἰησοῦν καὶ εἰς πάντας τοὺς ἁγίους, ⁶ ὅπως ἡ κοινωνία τῆς πίστεώς σου ἐνεργὴς γένηται ἐν ἐπιγνώσει παντὸς ἀγαθοῦ τοῦ ἐν ἡμῖν εἰς Χριστόν. ⁷ χαρὰν γὰρ πολλὴν ἔσχον καὶ παράκλησιν ἐπὶ τῇ ἀγάπῃ σου, ὅτι τὰ σπλάγχνα τῶν ἁγίων ἀναπέπαυται διὰ σοῦ, ἀδελφέ.

> ⁴*I thank my God always when I remember you in my prayers,* ⁵*because I hear of your love and of the faith which you have toward the Lord Jesus and all the saints,* ⁶*and I pray that the sharing of your faith may promote the knowledge of all the good that is ours in Christ.* ⁷*For I have derived much joy and comfort from your love, my brother, because the hearts of the saints have been refreshed through you.*

---

[4] See my comments on Phil 1:2 in *C-Phil*; Rom 1:7 in *C-Rom*; and Col 1:2 above.

Paul, as the high priest, raises his prayer of thanksgiving to God, the originator of all good and the one who brings to perfection (Phil 1:6) the love and faith exhibited by Philemon. The text at face value seems to indicate that both Philemon's faith and love are directed to the Lord Jesus and to all the saints. But such does not make sense since in the New Testament faith never has other human beings as its object. The explanation lies in reading Philemon 5 as an *inclusio* ABB'A', where the first element (love) has the last element (all the saints) as its object, whereas the second (faith) and third (the Lord Jesus) elements go together. This is corroborated in that the parallel statement in Colossians reads "because we have heard of your faith in Christ Jesus and of the love which you have for all the saints" (1:4).[5] Paul starts with love because love is ultimately the tangible reality (faith working through love; Gal 5:6) of the fellowship of those who have put their trust in the gospel (*koinōnia pisteōs*; Philem 6).[6] Fellowship is essentially full table fellowship, especially between Jew and Gentile, where the real test of love takes place.[7] Philemon 6 is a compact formula of what Paul developed in Philippians 1:3-11 and Colossians 1:9-10. The fellowship starts with the gospel to which we adhere by putting our trust in its teaching (Phil 1:5, 7), which summons us to do the good work of love in view of the day of the Lord (vv.6, 10).[8] This work of love is to be implemented mainly "among us (or you)" (*en hēmin* or *hymin*; Philem 6) as Paul indicated in Galatians 6:10: "So

---

[5] See my comments earlier on that verse.
[6] Notice how Philemon 6 corresponds to Galatians 5:6 terminology wise in that the fellowship of faith is made active (*energēs*; Philem 6) just as faith is said to be working (*energoumenē*) through love (Gal 5:6).
[7] See my comments on Gal 2:9-14 in *Gal*; Phil 1:1-11 in *C-Phil*; 2:1; Rom 12:13 and 15:26 in *C-Rom*.
[8] Notice that *eis Khriston* (unto/toward Christ; Philem 6) is a shortened formula for *eis hēmeran Khristou* (until the day of Christ; Phil 1:10).

then, as we have opportunity, let us do good to all men, and especially to those who are of the household of faith."[9] As explicated in Colossians, the "full knowledge (*epignōsei*) of every good (work)" (Philem 6) is secured through the full knowledge of God's will: "And so, from the day we heard of it, we have not ceased to pray for you, asking that you may be filled with the full knowledge (*epignōsin*) of his *will* in all spiritual wisdom and understanding, to lead a life worthy of the Lord, fully pleasing to him, bearing fruit *in every good work* and increasing in the full knowledge (*epignōsei*) of God." (Col 1:9-10). God's will is communicated to the brethren through the word of teaching from scripture which is the centerpiece of table fellowship.[10]

The centrality of love is further corroborated in that it is Philemon's love that provides joy and comfort to Paul. Together with peace, joy is a staple of the Jerusalem above and thus awaits us at the end of the path we have to tread according to God's will (Phil 1:25-26).[11] Consequently, whatever we may experience of that joy in the meantime, we do insofar as we behave as citizens of that heavenly city (1:27; 3:20). That is why, at the news that the gospel leading to God's kingdom is proclaimed, Paul exclaims: "and in that I rejoice. Yes, and I *shall rejoice.*" (1:18-19) The comfort (*paraklēsin*) that Paul reaps from Philemon's loving attitude toward his colleagues (Philem 7) is the consolation that is provided by the preaching and teaching of the gospel (Rom 12:8; 1 Cor 14:3, 31). Thus, essentially the consolation (*paraklēsis*) is something that God bestows through his gospel and, by the same token, something that Paul would

---

[9] Which makes the RSV translation of *pantos agathou tou en hēmin eis Khriston* as "all good that is ours in Christ" (v. 6) at best weak and at worst problematic and misleading.
[10] See *C-Phil* 58-68.
[11] Notice how the joy is subsequent to the progress on that path.

provide to Philemon and not vice versa. Still, since the preaching of God's will does not actually materialize as gospel (good news) unless and until it has borne fruit, the news of such functions as "gospel" for the apostle:

> But now that Timothy has come to us from you, and *has brought us the good news* (*evangelisamenou*) of your faith and love and reported that you always remember us kindly and long to see us, as we long to see you—for this reason, brethren, in all our distress and affliction *we have been comforted* (*pareklēthēmen*) about you through your faith; for now we live, if you stand fast in the Lord. (1 Thess 3:6-8)

That is also why, for Paul, "the *beginning* of the gospel" coincides with his leaving Macedonia, and not with his arrival there (Phil 4:15).

The close link of Philemon 6 to Philippians is confirmed by the similar terminology in Philemon 6-7 and Philippians 2:1-2:

> ... and I pray that the sharing (*koinōnia*; fellowship) of your faith may promote the knowledge of all the good that is ours in Christ. For I have derived much *joy* and comfort (*paraklēsin*) from your *love*, my brother, because the entrails (*splankhna*: wombs) of the saints have been refreshed through you. (Philem 6-7)

> So if there is any encouragement (*paraklēsis*) in Christ, any incentive (*paramythion*)[12] of *love*, any participation (*koinōnia*; fellowship) in the Spirit, any affection (*splankhna*) and sympathy, complete my *joy* by being of the same mind, having the same *love*, being in full accord and of one mind. (Phil 2:1-2)

---

[12] *paraklēsis* (exhortation) and *paramythion* (comfort) have a similar connotation and go together as is evident from 1 Cor 14:3: "On the other hand, he who prophesies speaks to men for their upbuilding and encouragement (*paraklēsin*) and consolation (*paramythian*)."

Furthermore, the parallelism between the two passages confirms that the point Paul is stressing in Philemon's behavior is love for the brethren, which the Apostle will use to pressure his addressee to accept the repentant Onesimus. Actually, this intent is confirmed by the use of *splankhna* (entrails, that is, the center of parental affection). Indeed, this same noun will appear twice again in Philemon 12 and 20, the second of which will be in conjunction with the same verb "refresh" that occurs in v.7. The link in thought between vv.7 and 20 is actually very strong, the former playing the role of *captatio benevolentiae* (tapping on the shoulder; positive reinforcement) in view of the difficult request in vv.17-20 that Philemon receive Onesimus without retaliation. One is reminded that scriptural love is not so much between equals, but rather toward those in need, and thus the loving care of a senior toward a junior who is in need of it. This explains why such love is an act of compassion and its source lies in the "entrails."[13] In v.7b, Paul cajoles Philemon by telling him that his behavior is a living example to the saints, especially those in position of authority, with the result being that his colleagues are refreshed (find solace) in his example while on the exacting path of scriptural love. This cajoling has its price in that, later in v.20a, Paul will ask Philemon to refresh him so that the Apostle's entrails might also find solace. Put otherwise, Paul is asking Philemon to be an example not only to the saints, but even to God's apostles!

---

[13] The classic example is Jesus' attitude toward the multitude that followed him and needed to be fed with his teaching as well as with food: "As he went ashore he saw a great throng, and he had compassion (*esplankhnisthē*; his entrails [womb] were moved) on them, because they were like sheep without a shepherd; and he began to teach them many things" (Mk 6:34); "I have compassion (*splankhnizomai*) on the crowd, because they have been with me now three days, and have nothing to eat." (8:2) The Greek verb is from the same root as *splankhna* (entrails).

Vv. 8-16 ⁸Διὸ πολλὴν ἐν Χριστῷ παρρησίαν ἔχων ἐπιτάσσειν σοι τὸ ἀνῆκον ⁹ διὰ τὴν ἀγάπην μᾶλλον παρακαλῶ, τοιοῦτος ὢν ὡς Παῦλος πρεσβύτης νυνὶ δὲ καὶ δέσμιος Χριστοῦ Ἰησοῦ· ¹⁰ παρακαλῶ σε περὶ τοῦ ἐμοῦ τέκνου, ὃν ἐγέννησα ἐν τοῖς δεσμοῖς, Ὀνήσιμον, ¹¹ τόν ποτέ σοι ἄχρηστον νυνὶ δὲ [καὶ] σοὶ καὶ ἐμοὶ εὔχρηστον, ¹² ὃν ἀνέπεμψά σοι, αὐτόν, τοῦτ᾽ ἔστιν τὰ ἐμὰ σπλάγχνα· ¹³ Ὃν ἐγὼ ἐβουλόμην πρὸς ἐμαυτὸν κατέχειν, ἵνα ὑπὲρ σοῦ μοι διακονῇ ἐν τοῖς δεσμοῖς τοῦ εὐαγγελίου, ¹⁴ χωρὶς δὲ τῆς σῆς γνώμης οὐδὲν ἠθέλησα ποιῆσαι, ἵνα μὴ ὡς κατὰ ἀνάγκην τὸ ἀγαθόν σου ᾖ ἀλλὰ κατὰ ἑκούσιον. ¹⁵ Τάχα γὰρ διὰ τοῦτο ἐχωρίσθη πρὸς ὥραν, ἵνα αἰώνιον αὐτὸν ἀπέχῃς, ¹⁶ οὐκέτι ὡς δοῦλον ἀλλ᾽ ὑπὲρ δοῦλον, ἀδελφὸν ἀγαπητόν, μάλιστα ἐμοί, πόσῳ δὲ μᾶλλον σοὶ καὶ ἐν σαρκὶ καὶ ἐν κυρίῳ.

> ⁸Accordingly, though I am bold enough in Christ to command you to do what is required, ⁹yet for love's sake I prefer to appeal to you—I, Paul, an ambassador and now a prisoner also for Christ Jesus—¹⁰I appeal to you for my child, Onesimus, whose father I have become in my imprisonment. ¹¹(Formerly he was useless to you, but now he is indeed useful to you and to me.) ¹²I am sending him back to you, sending my very heart. ¹³I would have been glad to keep him with me, in order that he might serve me on your behalf during my imprisonment for the gospel; ¹⁴but I preferred to do nothing without your consent in order that your goodness might not be by compulsion but of your own free will. ¹⁵Perhaps this is why he was parted from you for a while, that you might have him back for ever, ¹⁶no longer as a slave but more than a slave, as a beloved brother, especially to me but how much more to you, both in the flesh and in the Lord.

Now that he has set the stage through his *captatio benevolentiae*, Paul embarks on his plea by making Philemon an offer he could not refuse without incurring shame: how could Philemon, the paterfamilias who expects his subordinates to obey his will, refuse to obey Paul, his senior in the Lord? Indeed, right from the beginning, Paul states that his position allows him great boldness "in Christ" to "command" Philemon to do "what is required of him." And that would have been the end of the story. However he opts not to shame Philemon with the view of later asking him not to shame Onesimus. Actually, Paul's option is the way of love for which he has just praised Philemon, declaring him an example for the saints. In the name of that same love, Paul "appeals" to Philemon to implement his request. Still, his request is that of a senior, which basically amounts to an order.[14] Indeed, Paul is Philemon's "elder" (*presbytēs*),[15] worthy of the obedience as well as honor. What is amazing, though, is that Paul adds the mention of his being now a chained prisoner (*desmios*) for the sake of the Messiah Jesus, who is the ultimate Lord (v.3) beyond Philemon and even beyond Paul himself.[16] In so doing, Paul is not only using his own seniority and but also the lordship of Jesus as leverage against any possible complaint or even reticence on Philemon's part. Since he could have reached the same result by simply presenting himself as the apostle or even the slave of Christ, as he usually does, Paul must have had another reason for stressing the fact that besides being Philemon's senior, he is Christ's chained prisoner.[17] That the thought is foremost on his mind is evident in the initial greeting, introducing himself as "chained prisoner of the Christ Jesus" (v.1), a unique instance in the Pauline corpus.[18] Consequently, the mention of his being a chained prisoner in v.9 is not a mere aesthetic addition, but an

---

[14] See my comments on *erōtō* (ask, beseech, request) in *1 Thess* 133-4.

[15] *presbytēs* is the *lectio difficilior* (the reading more difficult to account for) and thus the original reading. *presbevtēs* (ambassador) is a conjectural emendation endorsed by RSV.

[16] A strategy similar to that found in Philippians where Paul introduces himself together with Timothy as Christ's slaves (1:1).

[17] Notice the underscoring expressed in the Greek *nyni de kai* (yet now, also [a prisoner]).

[18] The two other occurrences are found in the body of the letter (Philem 9; Eph 3:1). In Eph 4:1 we have "a chained prisoner in the Lord (*en Kyriō*)."

essential part of his argument. It immediately precedes the first reference to Onesimus, who is introduced as the child whom Paul begat "while in chains (*en desmois*)" (v.10) and who is the subject of Paul's request as is clear from the repetition of "I appeal" (*parakalō*) in v.9 at the beginning of v.10. On the other hand, since Paul's imprisonment is for the sake of Christ, that is, for the gospel (v.13; see also Eph 3:1-7), then Onesimus is the "brother" of Philemon (Philem 16), who is also Paul's child in the gospel (v.19b).

The Greek *Onēsimos* means "useful, profitable, beneficial, enjoyable." Paul will immediately use that meaning to his advantage in the argument of his letter. Indeed, the magisterial v. 11 reads: "Formerly he was useless (*akhrēston*) to you, but now he is indeed useful (*evkhrēston*) to you and to me." This statement is much weightier than meets the ear. First and foremost, there is the play on the meaning of *Onēsimos*. Secondly, the root of the Greek *akhrēston* and *evkhrēston* is *khrēstos* (benevolent) which sounds like *Khristos* (Christ). The assonance between the two is used throughout the New Testament with the intention of saying that being *khrēstos* (benevolent) is equivalent to be Christ-like and ultimately like God in his benevolence (*khrēstotēs*).[19]

Just as in v.11, the two relative clauses in vv.12 and 13 further elaborate on Onesimus in conjunction with both Paul and Philemon. It is as though the Apostle wants to offer the fugitive slave as the factual link bridging the physical distance between the free Philemon and the imprisoned Paul. The importance of this point lies in the fact that, should Paul not survive his stay in prison (Phil 1:21-23), Onesimus will prove to be the presence of

---

[19] See my comments on *khrēstologias* (Rom 16:18) in *C-Rom* 284.

"another Paul" for Philemon. Indeed, Paul writes that Onesimus is tantamount to "my own entrails" (*ta ema splankhna*), which is the seat of the love enjoined by the gospel (v.7). This metaphor is multi-faceted. It shows not only how dear Onesimus is in Paul's eyes but also that, should Philemon refuse to accept him, he would be refusing not only Paul himself but the latter's entrails. The consequence of such an action would be that Paul would not find rest (v.7b). More importantly, however, it would show that Philemon is lacking in the love for which Paul had just praised him (v.7a). Furthermore, in asking Philemon to accept the offer, Paul is actually taking the attitude of a junior toward a senior as witnessed in his "sending up"[20] (v.12) Onesimus to Philemon. This is in preparation for what he is about to write in v.14: that Paul is doing so only with Philemon's permission. However, this is obviously a literary device since Paul has already forced Philemon's hand by having sent (*anepempsa*) Onesimus with the letter.[21] This corresponds to our saying "Allow me to say…"; "If I may…"; "I hope I am not imposing…"; "With your permission, I am going to…" It is a "polite" way to do what one has embarked on doing or even has already done, especially in the case of writing when the addressee is not present to give or decline permission.

Paul is actually wielding a preemptive strike by putting the onus on Philemon with his "imposed" offer: Paul would have preferred to keep the much needed Onesimus with himself, however he is willing to sacrifice losing him for Philemon's sake! And Paul's reasoning is compelling. If Onesimus would have

---

[20] "I am sending him back" (RSV) is the translation of *anepempsa* from *anapempō* which literally means "send up."

[21] This is the literary "past tense." By the time Philemon is reading the letter, the action of sending is already in the past; so the Greek *anepempsa* actually means "I sent."

remained with Paul, he would have served the cause of the gospel on Philemon's behalf. Put otherwise, Philemon would have been spared the possibility of refusing Paul and, by the same token, would have "paid his debt to Paul" (v.19b) without any effort on his part, just by relinquishing his own slave to serve Paul's cause. Still, what is most impressive is that Paul uses the terminology of diaconal service at table fellowship (*diakonē*) to speak of Onesimus' work with Paul on Philemon's behalf. It is as though he is indirectly chiding Philemon, the paterfamilias who is attended to at table while Paul is in jail, for not having been himself the "deacon" serving the "high priest" Paul in his service of the gospel.[22] Philemon should have been sharing the chains with Paul, and yet it was Onesimus, the renegade, who was doing just that.

However, Paul insists that Philemon undergo out of his own free will, not through imposition, the test of doing the "good" (work) required by love (v.14; see vv.6-7), namely, to accept Onesimus as equal to himself, being a "brother" and a "fellow deacon." Here again, the writer proves masterful. Paul is saying obliquely that it behooves Philemon to accept the imposition of the fait accompli laid upon him by Paul so that he, Philemon, would not run the risk of missing the mark while exercising his free decision. This is borne out by the phraseology of v.14, "but I preferred to do nothing without your consent in order that your goodness might not be by compulsion (*kata anankēn*; out of [imposed] necessity) but of your own free will (*kata hekousion*)," which corresponds to the phraseology used in conjunction with the gospel's requirement:

---

[22] See my comments on Phil 2:17 in *C-Phil* 138-9 and on Rom 1:8 in *C-Rom* 43.

> For if I preach the gospel, that gives me no ground for boasting. For necessity (*anankē*) is laid upon me. Woe to me if I do not preach the gospel! For if I do this of my own will (*hekōn* [from the same root as *hekousion*]), I have a reward; but if not of my own will (*akōn*), I am entrusted with a commission. What then is my reward? Just this: that in my preaching I may make the gospel free of charge, not making full use of my right in the gospel. For though I am free from all men, I have made myself a slave to all, that I might win the more. (1 Cor 9:16-19)

It is then by *submitting willingly* to the gospel (Rom 1:5; 16:26) and its injunction of "doing good to all men, and especially to those who are of the household of faith" (Gal 6:10) that one is sure to pass the test. This is precisely why Paul was forcing Philemon's hand instead of allowing him too much latitude.

Still, all in all, Philemon is the big winner. Perhaps, writes Paul, there is a reason behind Onesimus' fleeing and thus "being taken away for a while" from Philemon: so that his master would receive him again "for good and ever" (*aiōnion*). Not only that, but Philemon will have gained not merely another slave, of which he has many, but rather a beloved brother both in the flesh and in the Lord (*kai en sarki kai en kyriō*). The last phrase brings to mind Colossians: "Slaves, obey in everything those who are your earthly (*kata sarka*) masters (*kyriois*: lords), not with eyeservice, as men-pleasers, but in singleness of heart, fearing the Lord (*ton kyrion*). Whatever your task, work heartily, as serving the Lord and not men, knowing that from the Lord you will receive the inheritance as your reward; you are serving the Lord Christ." (3:22-24) Thus, in Onesimus, Philemon will be gaining a brother who would never betray him, even as brothers might do, since Onesimus' obedience is bound, beyond Philemon, to the lordship of Christ whereby "the wrongdoer will be paid back for the wrong he has done, and *there is no partiality*" (Col 3:25).

How can Paul be sure that that will be the case? It is because Onesimus submitted freely and willingly to someone who is in chains and who is not his earthly master, and has proven to be a beloved brother.

Vv. 17-20 ¹⁷εἰ οὖν με ἔχεις κοινωνόν, προσλαβοῦ αὐτὸν ὡς ἐμέ. ¹⁸ εἰ δέ τι ἠδίκησέν σε ἢ ὀφείλει, τοῦτο ἐμοὶ ἐλλόγα. ¹⁹ ἐγὼ Παῦλος ἔγραψα τῇ ἐμῇ χειρί, ἐγὼ ἀποτίσω· ἵνα μὴ λέγω σοι ὅτι καὶ σεαυτόν μοι προσοφείλεις. ²⁰ ναὶ ἀδελφέ, ἐγώ σου ὀναίμην ἐν κυρίῳ· ἀνάπαυσόν μου τὰ σπλάγχνα ἐν Χριστῷ.

> ¹⁷*So if you consider me your partner, receive him as you would receive me.* ¹⁸*If he has wronged you at all, or owes you anything, charge that to my account.* ¹⁹*I, Paul, write this with my own hand, I will repay it—to say nothing of your owing me even your own self.* ²⁰*Yes, brother, I want some benefit from you in the Lord. Refresh my heart in Christ.*

This being the new situation, the onus of the test is now on Philemon who has to prove that he is Paul's "fellow" (*koinōnon*; partner): "*If therefore* (*Ei oun*) *you consider me your partner, receive him as you would receive me.*" He is to receive Onesimus as though he is receiving Paul himself, his *senior* partner in the fellowship of the gospel. The reason for this is that Onesimus, holder of Paul's letter, is his emissary and thus worthy of all honor,[23] especially that he is presented as "Paul's entrails," his innermost paternal—and thus authoritative—self (v.12). Nonetheless, Paul does not forget that, legally speaking, Onesimus is still Philemon's slave and as such he is indebted (*opheilei*) to Philemon for all damages that Philemon may have

---

[23] Mt 10:40 (He who receives you receives me, and he who receives me receives him who sent me). See also Gal 4:14 (and though my condition was a trial to you, you did not scorn or despise me, but received me as an angel of God, as Christ Jesus).

incurred due to Onesimus' long absence and possibly with any legal wrong (*ēdikēsen*) that absence may have caused Philemon (v.18a). The latter possibility may well have pertained in a court of law where Philemon could have charged Paul, a Roman citizen, of having given haven to someone else's fledgling slave and even adopted him, as Paul actually acknowledges in no uncertain terms in the letter. If so, then Paul's "charge that to my account (*elloga*)" (v.18b) may well be more than figurative style. Indeed, the verb used here *ellogō* occurs only once more in the New Testament with a clear legal connotation: "sin indeed was in the world before the law was given, but sin is *not counted* (*ellogeitai*) *where there is no law*." (Rom 5:13) Consequently, Paul may well have been defending himself rather than Onesimus here by accepting to take the blame and, by the same token, asking forgiveness from Philemon. If so, then Paul is putting the ultimate pressure on Philemon: a father (in Christ Jesus through the gospel; 1 Cor 4:15), not coming with a rod, but with love in a spirit of gentleness (v.21), and actually asking his son's forgiveness! How could Philemon, whose love was just highly praised (Philem 7), not be literally overwhelmed?

The legality of the tone of Philemon 18 is corroborated in v.19a where Paul seals in writing his promise to make compensation by repaying any damages with the phrase, "I, Paul, write this with my own hand." Yet, while telling Philemon that he is ready to pay any damages, Paul is quick to remind his addressee of the greater debt[24] he owes Paul, that is, his own self. Philemon, and for that matter, Onesimus, both became Paul's sons in the gospel and thus members of the Christian table fellowship as "brothers." That this thought is on Paul's mind is confirmed in the immediately following, "Yes, brother" (v.20a).

---

[24] *prosopheileis* actually means "owe besides, owe over and above."

It is further corroborated in that the "yes" (*nai*; indeed) is in view of underscoring that the *benefit* Paul is looking forward to *reap* (*onaimēn*) from Philemon is due him "in the Lord" (v.20b). The Greek speaking hearers could not miss the intentional use of the verb *onaimēn*, which is of the same root as *Onesimos*. So Paul is actually burdening Philemon with the extra debt (reflected in the verb *prosopheileis* in v.19) of being his "son" in the gospel over and above the debt of getting back Onesimus whom Paul could have kept. Then Paul overwhelms Philemon by asking him to refresh his "entrails" "in Christ" (v.20c), thus pressuring Philemon to live up to his fame (v.7).

However, there is more to the phrase, "I, Paul, write this with my own hand," than is evident. The expression "with my own hand" serves as the ending to a cluster of epistles: Romans and 1 Corinthians; 2 Corinthians and Galatians; Ephesians, Philippians, and Colossians; and 1 and 2 Thessalonians.[25] Consequently, its occurrence in Philemon 19a also serves, in a literary way, to hold together the four Pauline letters addressed to individuals.

Vv. 21-22 *²¹Πεποιθὼς τῇ ὑπακοῇ σου ἔγραψά σοι, εἰδὼς ὅτι καὶ ὑπὲρ ἃ λέγω ποιήσεις. ²²ἅμα δὲ καὶ ἑτοίμαζέ μοι ξενίαν· ἐλπίζω γὰρ ὅτι διὰ τῶν προσευχῶν ὑμῶν χαρισθήσομαι ὑμῖν.*

> ²¹*Confident of your obedience, I write to you, knowing that you will do even more than I say.* ²²*At the same time, prepare a guest room for me, for I am hoping through your prayers to be granted to you.*

And before allowing Philemon a breather to think over the entire matter, Paul expresses his confidence that Philemon will obediently submit to the gospel (Philem 21a), as all Roman

---

[25] 1 Cor 16:21; Gal 6:11; Col 4:18; 2 Thess 3:17.

citizens have been invited to do (Rom 1:5; 16:25). Furthermore, Paul is confident that Philemon will go beyond the call of that obedience and will do more than what Paul expects from him (21b). Finally and at the same time, Paul requests that Philemon prepare for him a *xenian* (literally hospitality, and thus a guest room) since he hopes that through the prayers of all the members of Philemon's household[26] he would be granted to be with them through God's grace[27] (v.22). Again, if this happens, then Paul's abiding in Philemon's household has two facets. First of all, it is an honor to Philemon that Paul would choose his household over any other residence. Secondly, being Philemon's senior, Paul's coming would amount to a visit by the emperor or a senator to a Roman patrician's home. The visitor, being the senior, would be seated at the head of the table, meaning that he would function as the host and consequently his will would prevail. By the same token, Paul's hoped for visit is the ultimate pressure put on Philemon to receive Onesimus, or else he will have to answer to his superior whenever the latter arrives.

Vv. 23-25 ²³ Ἀσπάζεταί σε Ἐπαφρᾶς ὁ συναιχμάλωτός μου ἐν Χριστῷ Ἰησοῦ, ²⁴ Μᾶρκος, Ἀρίσταρχος, Δημᾶς, Λουκᾶς, οἱ συνεργοί μου. ²⁵ Ἡ χάρις τοῦ κυρίου Ἰησοῦ Χριστοῦ μετὰ τοῦ πνεύματος ὑμῶν.

> ²³ *Epaphras, my fellow prisoner in Christ Jesus, sends greetings to you,*
> ²⁴ *and so do Mark, Aristarchus, Demas, and Luke, my fellow workers.*
> ²⁵ *The grace of the Lord Jesus Christ be with your spirit.*

In the final greetings, Paul names five "fellow-workers": Epaphras, Mark, Aristarchus, Demas, and Luke (vv.23-24). These same names are found in Colossians 4:10-14. Similar to

---

[26] "Your" (*hymōn*) is in the plural.
[27] Which is the meaning of the Greek *kharisthēsomai hymin* (I shall be "graced" upon you).

Colossians, Epaphras is introduced at length. The reason is to put the mighty Archippus in his shadow. In Colossians, the "deacon" Archippus (4:17) is to follow in the footsteps of the "deacon" Epaphras (1:7).[28] Here also, Paul's "fellow soldier" Archippus will always have to remember that the greetings addressed to Philemon's household of which he is a member (Philem 2) originate not only from Paul and Timothy (v.1) but also from Epaphras, Paul's "fellow prisoner (fellow exile)" who is thus equal to Paul in his "chains" (v.1), a status that Archippus has still to attain.

And, again, as is classic in Paul's letters, after having begun by wishing Philemon and his household continual grace and the peace (v.3), he closes his letter by wishing them the grace (v.25) of the Lord Jesus Christ so that, at the end of the way, they may attain salvation and the peace of the Kingdom (Rom 5:1-11).

---

[28] See above my comments on Col 4:17.

Further Reading

Commentaries and Studies

John Chrysostom, Homilies on Colossians in P. Schaff, ed., *The Nicene and Post-Nicene Fathers*. Grand Rapids, 1st Series, xiii 1979: 257-321.

John Chrysostom, Homilies on Philemon in P. Schaff, ed., *The Nicene and Post-Nicene Fathers*. Grand Rapids, 1st Series, xiii 1979: 547-557.

Aletti, J.-N. *Saint Paul: Epître aux Colossiens. Introduction, traduction et commentaire*. Etudes Bibliques, nouvelle série 20. Paris: Gabalda, 1993.

Barclay, J. M. G. *Colossians and Philemon*. T&T Clark Study Guides. London-New York: T&T Clark International, 2004.

Barth, M. and Blanke, H. *The Letter to Philemon. A New Translation with Notes and Commentary*. Eerdmans Critical Commentary. Grand Rapids–Cambridge, UK: Eerdmans, 2000.

Fitzmyer, J. A. *The Letter to Philemon. A New Translation with Introduction and Commentary*. Anchor Bible, 34C. New York–London: Doubleday, 2000.

Harrington, D. J. *Paul's Prison Letters. Spiritual Commentaries on Paul's Letters to Philemon, the Philippians, and the Colossians*. Hyde Park, NY: New City, 1997.

Hay D. M. *Colossians*. Abingdon NT Commentaries. Nashville, TN: Abingdon, 2000.

MacDonald, M.Y. *Colossians and Ephesians*. Sacra Pagina, 17. Collegeville MN: Liturgical Press, 2000.

Martin, R. P. *Ephesians, Colossians, and Philemon*. Interpretation: Anchor Bible Commentary for Teaching and Preaching. Atlanta: Knox, 1991.

Nordling, J. G. *Philemon*. Concordia Commentary. St Louis, MO: Concordia, 2004.

Osiek, C. *Philippians, Philemon*. Abingdon New Testament Commentaries. Nashville, TN: Abingdon, 2000.

Thompson, N. M. *Colossians and Philemon*. Two Horizons New Testament Commentary. Grand Rapids–Cambridge, UK: Eerdmans, 2005.

Thurston, B. B. and Ryan, J. M. *Philippians and Philemon*. Sacra Pagina, 10. Collegeville, MN: Liturgical Press, 2005.

Wall, R. W. *Colossians and Philemon*. IVP New Testament Commentary. Downers Grove, IL–Leicester, UK: InterVarsity, 1993.

Walsh, B. J. and Keesmat, S. C. *Colossians Remixed. Subverting the Empire*. Downers Grove, IL–Leicester, UK: InterVarsity, 2004. A must read.

Wengst K. *Der Brief an Philemon*. Theologischer Kommentar zum Neuen Testament, 16. Stuttgart: Kohlhammer, 2005.

Wilson, R. M. *A Critical and Exegetical Commentary on Colossians and Philemon*. International Critical Commentary. London–New York: T&T Clark, 2005.

Articles

Barclay, J. M. G. "Paul, Philemon, and the Dilemma of Christian Slave-Ownership." *New Testament Studies* 37 (1991) 161-186.

Birdsall, J. N. "Πρεσβύτης in Philemon 9: A Study in Conjectural Emendation." *New Testament Studies* 39 (1993) 625-630.

Heil, J. P. "The Chiastic Structures and Meaning of Paul's Letter to Philemon." *Biblica* 82 (2001) 178-206.

Rapske, B. M. "The Prisoner Paul in the Eyes of Onesimus." *New Testament Studies* 37 (1991) 187-203.

Slater, T. B. "Translating Col 1,2 and Eph 1,1." *Biblica* 87 (2006) 52-54.
Steyn, G. J. "Some Figures of Style in the Epistle to Philemon: Their Contribution towards the Persuasive Nature of the Epistle." *Ekklesiastikos Pharos* 77, (2005) 64-68. Imperative to read.
Swart, G. J. "Eschatological Vision or Exhortation to Visible Christian Conduct? Notes on the Interpretation of Colossians 3:4." *Neotestamentica* 33 (1999) 169-77. Opts for the latter.
Van Broekhoven, H. "The Social Profiles in the Colossian Debates." *Journal for the Study of the New Testament* 66 (1997) 73-90.

www.ingramcontent.com/pod-product-compliance
Lightning Source LLC
LaVergne TN
LVHW011400080426
835511LV00005B/357